Dr. Gerd Heuschmann

My Horse is in Front of the Vertical!

Ethical Horsemanship for a New Generation

Illustrated by Katharina Rücker-Weininger
Translated by Richard F. Williams

Xenophon Press

COPYRIGHT

This Edition: *My Horse is in Front of the Vertical! Ethical Horsemanship for a New Generation*

ISBN: 9781948717670

Copyright © 2025 Xenophon Press. All rights reserved.
www.XenophonPress.com
Franktown, Virginia 23354, USA

Translation, Editing and Artistic Direction: Richard F. Williams
Layout and Design: Robert Ashbaugh

All rights reserved. No part of this publication may be reproduced, distributed, or transmitted in any form or by any means, including photocopying, recording, or other electronic or mechanical methods, without the prior written permission of the publisher and the author, except in the case of brief quotations used in critical reviews and certain other non-commercial uses permitted by copyright law.

Any use of this publication for the training of generative artificial intelligence ("AI") technologies is expressly prohibited. The author and publisher reserve all rights to license the use of this work for training generative AI and the development of machine learning language models.

Riders should always ensure they are wearing appropriate safety gear: riding boots, gloves, and if necessary, body protectors. The publisher also recommends a properly fitted safety helmet that meets at least the EN1384/BSEN1384 or PAS015 standard.

Original German Edition:

Bibliographic Information of the German National Library:
The German National Library lists this publication in the German National Bibliography. Detailed bibliographic data can be accessed online at: https://d-nb.info/99600064X
ISBN 978-3930953509

Author: Dr. med. vet. Gerd Heuschmann
Publisher: Isabella Sonntag
Project Composition: Ellen Ruten

© 2010 Wu Wei Verlag e.K., 86938 Schondorf

2nd Edition – All rights reserved – ISBN 978-3930953509

Publisher's Introduction

First published in 2010, as *Mein Pferd hat die Nase Vorn!* (*My Horse is in Front of the Vertical!*) for the German-speaking horseworld, Gerd Heuschmann's work contains essential reading for anyone involved in the horse industry worldwide. This is why we are bringing it to the English language: because the message needs to be understood by all equestrians. The world of equestrian sport is often shaped by competing influences—fame, profit, ego, and other less noble motivations—that can obscure the true essence of ethicsl horsemanship: placing the well-being of our horses, as athletes and companions, above all else.

Throughout history, horses have played an unparalleled role in human civilization. They have been indispensable partners in transportation, industry, culture, education, leisure, and as loyal companions. Their contributions are immeasurable, and it is our responsibility to honor their legacy, preserve the integrity of horsemanship, and protect their welfare.

This book offers a clear, practical approach to riding, horse care, stabling, management, and training. It provides owners, trainers, instructors, breeders, parents, and—most importantly—riders of all ages with a logical framework for the proper treatment of horses. While Heuschmann's fact-based insights may seem intuitive to experienced equestrians, newcomers to the sport, hobby, or competitive riders often struggle to determine whether a trainer's methods, stable practices, or riding philosophy truly prioritize the horse's well-being. This book serves as a valuable guide to identifying and preserving the proven traditions of classical riding while providing guidelines for avoiding harmful practices.

Especially helpful are the three checklists that allow readers to assess instruction, stable management, and their own riding on a relative scale. These tools empower riders, parents, trainers, and breeders to analyze existing practices, identify areas for improvement, and implement positive, targeted changes in their daily equestrian activities.

At Xenophon Press, we are passionate about the ongoing education of riders in their pursuit of truth and excellence in horsemanship. If you find this book valuable, we would appreciate your positive review and your recommendation to fellow equestrians, students, and newcomers to the horse world.

With best regards,

Richard F. Williams
Translator/Editor/Publisher, Xenophon Press

Table of Contents

Copyright I
Publisher's Introduction II
Introduction 4
Words from the Author 5

Chapter 1 — Finger on the Wound
A Look Behind the Scenes................................ 7
The Riders.. 8
The Recreational Riders..................................... 9
The Competitive Riders..................................... 10
The Horse Breeders.. 12
The Spectators.. 14
The Judges... 16
The Riding Instructors and Riding Clubs........ 18

Chapter 2 – Classical Horsemanship
What Is It?... 21
The Army Riding Regulation............................ 22
The Ethical Principles of the FN....................... 24
With Calm and Time.. 25
Relaxation... 27
The Rider's Aids... 28

Chapter 3 – Your Horse's Environment
How Horses Want to Live.................................. 30
The Horse as a Flight Anima............................. 32
How Horses Should Live.................................... 35
Three Things Your Horse Needs....................... 36
Responsibility... 38

Chapter 4 – The Horse's Body
The Anatomy of Your Horse.............................. 41
The Bridge Structure.. 41
The Head.. 42
The Cervical Spine.. 42
The Thoracic Spine... 43
The Thoracic Vertebra.. 43
The Lumbar Vertebra... 43
The Sacrum.. 44
The Tail (Coccygeal) Vertebrae......................... 44
The Nuchal Ligament... 45
The Supraspinous Ligament.............................. 45
Muscles... 46
Skeletal Muscles.. 48
The Long Back Muscle....................................... 49
The Horse's Back... 50
The Loose Back... 51
The Supported Back... 52
The Tense Back.. 52
The Lower Tension Chain.................................. 53

The Neck Muscles.. 54
The Croup and Hindquarters.................................. 58
The Horse's Body and What Happens During Riding
– Natural Posture.. 61
The Stretching Posture.. 63
The Basic Gaits... 65
Problems Caused by the Rider............................... 68
The Head-Neck Axis... 69

CHAPTER 5 – TRAINING HORSES
With Patience and Calm.. 75
The Training Scale.. 76
Contact... 80
Young Horses... 84
Impulsion.. 86
How to Train Properly... 86
Lateral Movements... 88
Leg-Yielding.. 90
What Is Collection?... 91
The Influence of Your Horse's Conformation
on Its Training... 94
The Head Must Go Down?!.................................... 96
Not in the Mood?.. 98

CHAPTER 6 – YOU AND YOUR HORSE
Everything That Can Make You and Your Horse Happy 101
Basics – What You Need... 102
The Pasture Is Best – The Open Stall..................... 104
The Wealth of Your Options................................... 106
Healthy and Well-Groomed.................................... 108
Dressage Riding... 110
Show Jumping.. 112
Cavalletti Work... 115
Cross-Country and Eventing................................... 116
Hacking Out.. 119
Grazing and Walks.. 120
Driving a Sulky... 123
Mounted Games... 124
Groundwork.. 127
The Nine Ethical Principles of the Horse Friend.... 130

LIST OF ILLUSTRATIONS, PHOTOGRAPHS, AND DIAGRAMS 132
OTHER WORKS BY GERD HEUSCHMANN 132
REFLECTIONS 133
XENOPHON PRESS LIBRARY 136
THE CHECKLIST – YOUR RIDING INSTRUCTOR 140
THE ANSWERS – YOUR RIDING INSTRUCTOR 141
THE CHECKLIST – YOUR HORSE 142
THE ANSWERS – YOUR HORSE 143
THE CHECKLIST – YOUR STABLE 144
THE ANSWERS – YOUR STABLE 145
BIOGRAPHY OF THE AUTHOR 146

During the creation phase of this book, it became increasingly clear to us that we needed a central character—someone who could show you how your ponies and horses can *have the nose in front of the vertical.*

We needed a girl who is already on that path.

Gerd Heuschmann was thrilled when the illustrator suggested **Luise Foris**.

Luise is just such a girl. Of course, she still makes mistakes, and not everything is as perfect as she would like it to be—but for her, the well-being of her ponies always comes first.

And turning riding into an art form...
That is her greatest dream.

INTRODUCTION

There are approximately 60 million horses worldwide with an estimated 300,000 wild horses, leaving a significant portion of the total considered domesticated. A great deal of money is made with horses: breeders, dealers, equipment manufacturers, and many others generate approximately billions of dollars from the horse industry. The global economic impact of the equestrian sports (including competitive and leisure riding, but excluding racing) is around $300 billion annually.

That is an incredible amount of money! Some people deal with horses solely to make money or to be successful in competitions.

Sometimes, winning becomes more important than the love for the horse. As a result, horses are often trained poorly and too quickly, and ridden in completely incorrect ways. Their heads are pulled down in hopes of achieving fast results.

Another group of riders engages with horses purely for leisure and enjoyment. In that realm, many mistakes are made in care, feeding, and training. The main reason is a lack of knowledge.

Keep reading—and be part of the solution!

Dear Readers,

"My horse is in front of the vertical!" — this sentence holds many important meanings. The most important, of course, is that we can only truly train our horses well if they consistently carry their noses in front of the vertical.

If you succeed in riding your horse this way, you can also *have the nose in front of the vertical* in competition—with a healthy horse. But everything we will talk about in this book only works **if your horse has the nose in front of the vertical while you are riding**—which means that you must truly respect and love your horse. Otherwise, your horse becomes a slave.

The veterinarian who speaks for the horses.

In this book, I've tried to share a few thoughts that I believe are essential foundations for good riding. It doesn't matter whether you want to ride for fun out in the countryside, over jumps at a show, or within the dressage arena.

If you seriously dedicate yourself to horse training, for many of you, it will become a lifelong passion.

As a veterinarian who speaks for the horses, I can tell you from my own experience: **Always stay kind, open-minded, and curious.** Try to gather as much knowledge as you can to find the most horse-friendly path to training.

It's a lifelong journey—one of the most beautiful there is.

Yours truly,
Gerd Heuschmann

P.S. It's worth looking **beyond your own discipline**—toward other riding styles and training philosophies. The search for the most beautiful, effortless, and horse-respecting way to train is a lifelong pursuit.

My pony is happy to go to the show with me.

Even though the horse should engage a bit more from behind, it moves in a nice self-carriage with its nose in front of the vertical.

Chapter 1

Finger on the Wound
A Look Behind the Scenes

A lot of money is made with horses, and many people are involved in it. Not all of them treat horses well:

- Some riders handle their horses roughly and without consideration in order to achieve show success.
- There are breeders who want to make money quickly and therefore start young horses very early and rush their training.
- And there are competition judges who allow roughly trained horses to win.

These people harm the horses. Read the following pages and you'll understand why many things need to change.

Praise is the most important learning aid for your horse.

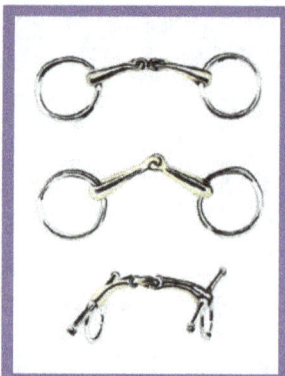

There are so many different types of bits. But the most important thing for your horse is **how** it is used. That's why you should always ride with a gentle, sensitive hand!

THE RIDERS

There are about 1.6 million riders in Germany (including children up to 14 years old). That's how many people regularly ride their own or others' horses. Some of them ride better, some not as well—but most of them try to treat their horses well.

Almost all of these riders ride, vault, or drive horses in their free time. Many riders are members of a riding club that is affiliated with the German Equestrian Federation (FN).

[Although many of the horse industry statistics in the original German edition of this book were for Germany, there is corresponding data for all first world nations. The important messages of Dr. Heuschmann are relevant to all equestrians worldwide. - Editor's note.]

Two friends after work.

The Recreational Riders

Riders who are not part of an FN-affiliated club and who do not compete in FN-sanctioned shows are usually referred to as recreational riders. These are riders who do not participate in dressage or show jumping competitions. Many of them primarily ride out into the countryside, while others follow dressage principles based on Spanish, Portuguese, or French traditions. Their role models come from so-called classical riding schools, such as those taught by Baucher and De la Guérinière [*École de Cavalerie Expanded Edition*, Xenophon Press 2015].

Most recreational riders strive for horse-friendly training. However, in this sector, there are many riding instructors with limited qualifications because they themselves have not received proper education. As a result, it is not always possible to judge whether their training methods are truly horse-friendly.

The riders themselves do not wish to harm their horses—they love horses and try to ride them as appropriately and humanely as possible. But mistakes are often made, not out of malice, but because they do not know everything that their horse needs. Many of these riders also don't know how or where to seek further education.

Who was Baucher?

François Baucher (1796–1873) was a Frenchman who published a new riding theory called *"Methods of Equitation According to New Principles."* His approach turned the prevailing ideas of his time upside down. Baucher's methods were, and still are, controversial because many misunderstood his concept of refined, light riding.

Baucher placed great emphasis on gentle and subtle influence on the horse and developed specific stretching exercises to release tension. However, if these exercises are applied incorrectly or excessively, they can also cause harm. His critics further argue that his horses did not move correctly over the back.

Often, for example, the noseband is fastened too tightly, which hinders the horse's ability to chew. In many cases, it can be left off entirely or at least buckled very loosely.

Who is De la Guérinière?

François Robichon de la Guérinière lived from 1688 to 1751 and is credited with inventing the riding seat that is still commonly used today. His non-violent training philosophy, *École de Cavalerie* [*École de Cavalerie Expanded Edition*, Xenophon Press 2015], describes the systematic schooling of the horse and is considered a foundational work of classical equestrian theory.

Guérinière is also regarded as the inventor of shoulder-in on the straight line, an exercise that is crucial for straightening the horse. This French master coined the phrase, "Dressage is for the horse, not the horse for dressage," thereby setting a groundbreaking standard for respectful and horse-friendly training.

The Competitive Riders

Many riders regularly compete in shows. Their motivation is success. But sometimes, in the pursuit of that success, the most important partner—the horse—is forgotten.

Competitive riding should serve as a test of proper training. That is its true purpose. The horse and its well-being must never be pushed into the background.

When horses lack correct training as riding horses, they suffer the most in the pursuit of victory. Added to this is the stress

Not like this!

But like this:

that arises for the horse when it is taken to competitions every single weekend.

These horses often become ill: incorrect riding overstrains their backs and legs; after a while, they need treatment from a veterinarian or even end up in a veterinary clinic.

> ## COMPETITION SPORT IN NUMBERS
> IN THE YEAR 2007 ...
> ... there were **1,409,834 competition starts.**
> IN THE YEAR 2008 ...
> ... there were **1,487,710 Competition starts.**
> That's almost **80,000 more starts** than the previous year.

Of course, the riders are not solely to blame:

An equestrian federation that organizes such competitions and allows young horses to compete too frequently plays just as much a role as the judges who award placements to incorrectly ridden horses.

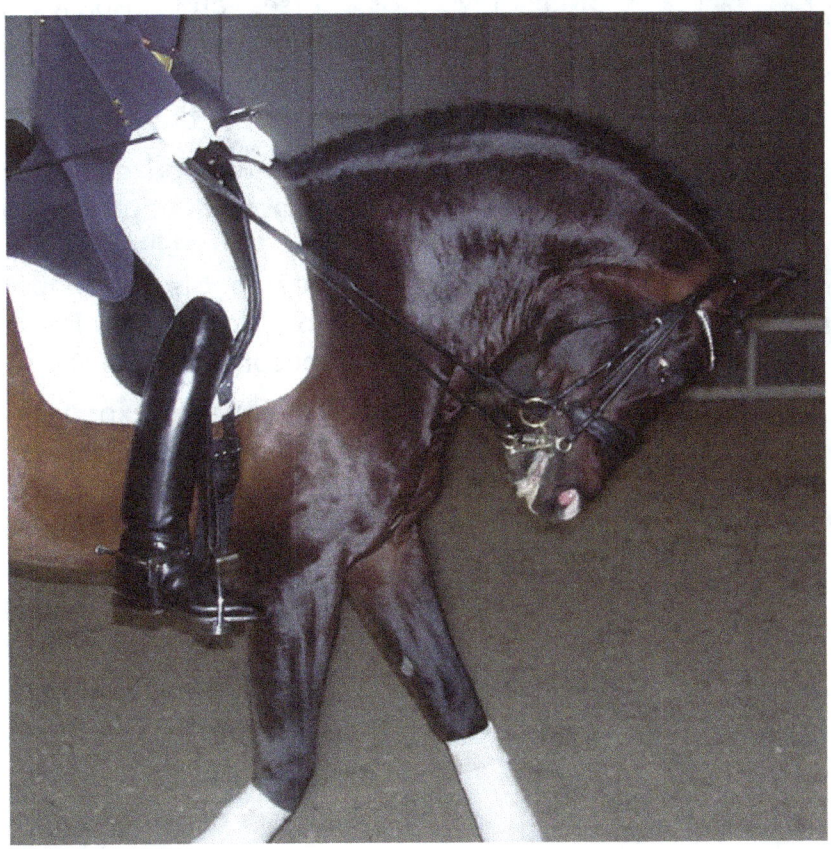

Images like this are unfortunately often seen in the warm-up area at competitions. This position causes the horse a great deal of pain.

A young horse, just like you, needs friends to feel comfortable.

The Horse Breeders

Without horse breeders, we wouldn't have all our beautiful horses. With great love for horses—and usually a wealth of knowledge about genetics, bloodlines, health, and raising foals—countless breeders pursue their passion.

Because horses with prizewinning parents or those with movement promising success in competition can sell for large sums of money, breeding is no longer done solely out of love for horses. Horse breeding has also become big business.

Raising and training horses is expensive. The earlier a breeder can sell a young horse as a promising competition prospect, the sooner their investment pays off—and the greater the profit. Since breeders, of course, need to make a living, there's nothing inherently wrong with approaching breeding from an economic standpoint.

However, the welfare of the young horses must never be pushed aside!

But some breeders want to earn as much as possible, as quickly as possible, and they try to sell their horses very young and for the highest

HORSE BREEDING IN GERMANY

IN THE YEAR 2008 ...

...1,204 riding horses were auctioned at an average price of just over 22,968 euros. In the past two years, both figures have declined significantly.

possible price—which comes at the expense of the horses.

The training of young horses often suffers.

Two- and three-year-old horses are often not started slowly and gently. They are not given enough time to get used to the rider's weight and to the demands of being a riding horse. Instead, they are expected to show spectacular movement at a very early age, with their heads fixed in place. Unfortunately, this is where many serious mistakes are made. These young horses are turned into *"correction cases"* early on and suffer consequences that last their entire lives.

This whole *"game"* only works because there are riders who are willing to buy such horses—and those riders still exist.

Sadly, they are willing to pay far less for a young horse that has been carefully and gently started than for one that already looks *ready for its first competition* and *flails its legs around* (see page 68, left-hand image).

They are hoping for quick competition success.

The little foals are in good hands with their mama.

The Spectators

Every competition always includes spectators. They cheer and applaud—and in doing so, they also influence which training methods are seen as successful.

Anyone who applauds a rider who not only rides poorly but even torments their horse through flashy but harmful riding, is, in a way, contributing to the spread of incorrect training methods. They share part of the blame when poor riding continues to be rewarded and becomes more widespread.

But how can one know when a horse is being ridden incorrectly?

Of course, not every spectator can recognize that right away. First, one has to learn—and that's not so easy—what a correctly ridden horse should look like. Very often, it's hard to tell from the outside whether a horse is well trained or poorly trained.

This book aims to provide you with important information to help you understand the difference.

Public interest reflects the great importance of competitive equestrian sport.

The Competition Judges

Winning a show with a poorly ridden horse? Is that even possible? Unfortunately, yes!

In today's equestrian sport—and this applies just as much to a small local show as it does to the Olympics—it is often the horses that "flail" stiffly through the dressage arena that end up being successful.

Even though this is completely wrong and harms the horse's health, it is still being presented—and rewarded.

Not like this!

But like this:

And if you can win at the Olympics riding like that, then this style of riding can't be all that bad, right? Many riders don't even realize that it is clearly wrong. And that's no surprise—because at many competitions, it's exactly these horses that receive the highest awards.

Judges reward the flashy front-leg flailing, regardless of how much the poor horse's back and neck might be in pain.

The criteria for good riding, as outlined by the German Equestrian Federation (FN) in the Guidelines for Riding and Driving, the Training

COMPETITION JUDGES IN GERMANY

Competition judges must complete basic training and pass an exam. To be admitted to this exam, they must provide proof of their own success in competitions.

Scale, and their Ethical Principles, often seem to be ignored.

That horses can win at shows when ridden this way is truly troubling. It leads more and more people to ride their horses incorrectly—they simply imitate the stars:

"If they can ride like that at major competitions and win, then it must be right..."

Judges play a critical role in shaping how people ride.

The well-being of competition horses lies especially in the hands of these three judges.

A good and sensitive riding instructor is absolutely essential!

THE RIDING INSTRUCTORS AND RIDING CLUBS

*Wearing a helmet is mandatory!
A good instructor always ensures that their students wear proper safety gear! The author and the publisher strongly recommend the use of properly fitted, approved safety helmets and equipment for all equestrian activities.*

Riding instructors and trainers determine how a horse is trained. They are often judged by how successful they are in competitions.

And an instructor or trainer whose horses do not place highly in shows is generally not considered successful. This puts riding instructors and trainers in a tough position.

Many of them know how to train horses correctly and in a horse-friendly way, but ultimately, they have to earn a living.

When clients demand quick success at the expense of the horse, trainers are sometimes forced to train the horses roughly and too quickly in order to meet those expectations.

Others have no proper education at all, yet call themselves "classical" or even "especially horse-friendly," when in reality, they lack real knowledge about horse care and training. These so-called instructors and trainers also cause harm.

So you should always ask your instructor about their qualifications—and not judge them only by show results or flashy riding displays.

You'll find a checklist at the end of this book to help you figure out whether you're in good hands with your riding instructor.

Summary
Finger on the Wound

The Rider

Why do you want to learn to ride, or why do you ride? Surely because you like horses! That may seem obvious to you, but it's important to emphasize—because success in competition should never become more important than your love and respect for the horse.

The Competitive Rider

Do you ride in competitions or hope to one day compete? That's not a bad thing—it's fun to experience something together with your horse and your friends.

But never forget that your horse should enjoy it too, and that it is not a sports machine. Only compete in a way that does not hurt your horse or overwhelm it.

Breeders

Maybe one day you'll get to choose your own horse from a breeder. If so, make sure the breeder loves horses as much as you do, and that your horse isn't too young to be ridden. Sometimes it's even better to buy an older, already trained horse—especially if you're still gaining experience.

Spectators

If you enjoy going to shows and watching, pay attention to how the horses are being ridden. You don't want to applaud someone who is hurting their horse, right?

Riding Instructors

A good riding instructor or trainer is probably the most important part of learning to ride. They can tell you exactly what to do to ride correctly and not hurt the horse. They will also help you train your horse so that it learns to carry you properly.

Classical horsemanship always draws on the proven experience of many generations of riders—and, of course, on the well-being of our horses. (This rider should be wearing a helmet.)

Chapter 2
Classical Horsemanship
What is it?

Have you ever read a book about learning to ride? These books are often titled something like *"Riding Instruction for Beginners"* and explain what you need to know about riding and the use of aids. That's a good thing, because with the help of such books, you can review at home what your riding instructor has explained, and find out, for example, why certain aids need to be given in specific ways.

On such a solid foundation, built with patience and time, true "horsemanship as an art form" can develop over many years. Only very sensitive, educated, and mature individuals can reach this highest goal.

There are many differences between various riding methods, but most of them are based on "classical horsemanship."

Any training philosophy that puts the horse's well-being and willingness to perform at its center can call itself "classical horsemanship."

It should also be traceable to a historical tradition.

The Army Service Regulations

The foundation of "Classical Equestrianism," which underlies our competitive riding, is the Army Service Regulations of 1912 (*H.Dv. 12 with Commentary,* Xenophon Press 2025). They were written for soldiers almost 100 years ago. *H.Dv. 12* contains the most important principles of training, such as:

> ### From Army Riding Regulation 12:
> "Purpose and principles of dressage: ... Its goal is to train the horse to the highest level of performance and to make it obedient. This goal can only be achieved if the horse—while preserving and developing its natural abilities—is brought into a form and posture that allows it to fully express its strength."

This old wording clearly states that the horse is at the center of training, not any particular training method. It's important to take into account the individual physical characteristics of each horse! That should really go without saying. After all, we know from our own experience that some things come easily to one person, while another may need more time.

If you had to summarize the quote from *H.Dv.12* in one sentence, it would be: "In the training of horses, consideration must always be given to the horse!"

Every horse can be ridden classically—including the PRE stallion shown here.

    This means that riding theory must always take into account the physical and mental foundation of the horse, and of course, the individual differences between horses must also be respected. After all, not all horses are the same—what comes easily to one may be difficult for another. In that regard, horses are no different from us! That's why a training method should never rigidly insist on its rules but must consider how the horse feels. In classical horsemanship, this is implicitly understood.

From the Ethical Principles of the FN

"The use of the horse in riding, driving, and vaulting must be based on its natural abilities, its capacity for performance, and its willingness to perform."

The Ethical Principles of the FN

The demand to adapt the pace of training to the horse in order not to overwhelm it is found not only in the *H.Dv.12 with Commentary*, Xenophon Press 2025, it is also clearly stated in the "Ethical Principles" of the German Equestrian Federation (FN), published in 1995, that consideration must be given to the horse in both riding and driving.

This means that the foundations of our modern riding methods—and in competitive sport itself—are intended to be horse-friendly.

Anyone who ignores this is not only violating the old classical teachings and the *H.Dv.12 with Commentary*, but also the current official guidelines set by the German Equestrian Federation.

A horse balanced in collection.

With Calm and Time

Much of what we do in life is done quickly and under pressure. We're often in a hurry—and that leads to stress.

But when dealing with horses, that doesn't work at all. Horses need calm and patience, and anyone who is rushed or hectic will quickly make a horse nervous. Stress and pressure undermine the rider's ability to develop a supple seat.

Calmness and patience are essential in the pursuit of classical horsemanship.

> ## THIS IS WHAT RIDING MASTER ALOIS PODHAJSKY SAYS:
>
> "Horse training cannot and must not proceed too quickly, otherwise the horse is at risk of health problems!"

This is how Colonel Alois Podhajsky, director of the famous Spanish Riding School in Vienna from 1939 until 1965, put it:

"I have time. – I want to call out this phrase to all riders who suddenly run into difficulties and can no longer find harmony with their horses."

With this, Alois Podhajsky points out one of the most important principles of all: Horse training must not be rushed, or else the horse will become tense and unhealthy. Young horses must be slowly and gradually accustomed to the rider's weight or else they develop back pain. Their muscles need time to adapt to this new form of stress.

A well-balanced horse – but unfortunately, it is resisting contact. You can see this because the right ear is held lower than the left—a clear sign that the horse is not evenly supple and through.

Training a young horse into a riding horse that can later compete takes several years. Anyone who demands difficult movements too early from their horse is overwhelming it. Even in everyday handling, calm and time are essential. Horses are flight animals, and rushed, hectic handling can make them insecure and fearful.

Relaxation (*Losgelassenheit*)

A very important concept that is repeatedly emphasized in classical riding theory is *Losgelassenheit*—relaxation or supple looseness.

If you've already taken riding lessons or earned a riding badge, you may have heard the term. It is part of the Training Scale (more on that on page 74), and thus a foundational principle of all horse training.

Learning to move relaxed under a rider is something young horses must first develop. They need time and practice to adjust to carrying a rider's weight. This is not easy and requires time and is emphasized in *The H.Dv.12 with Commentary*.

That manual also explains how a horse should move under a rider in order to stay healthy.

Riding Master Oskar Maria Stensbeck (1858 - 1939) said:

(One of the most important trainers of professional riders)

"If you are not able to make your horse even, yielding, and supple, then you should forgo all movements that can only be achieved in the highest degree of collection—rather than present them in a caricatured manner."

"The horse should learn to rediscover the posture it has achieved without a rider and to move freely under the rider's weight with a long neck and lowered nose." When a young horse—or a horse in the loosening phase—moves under the rider so relaxed and naturally on the aids, it is considered supple (*losgelassen*):

"Supple relaxation is recognized by the fact that the horse moves forward in trot with rhythm, reach, and without rushing, and shows the desire to stretch its neck forward and downward toward the accepting hand, that it swings elastically from the back, and carries its tail naturally and without tension."

THE RIDER'S AIDS

The aids serve as a means of communication between human and horse. They include the leg aids, rein aids, and weight aids.

The greatest focus in your training should be on developing a supple seat, as it is the most important and subtle way to communicate with your horse.

The most common mistakes are a harsh, backward-acting hand and a gripping, stiff, driving seat.

A well-ridden horse responds to the supple seat with the lightest rein influence and to the sensitive driving leg; there is no place for roughness here! Only in exceptional situations and emergencies should the reins be used as a means of discipline or as an "emergency brake."

A well-trained horse performs dressage movements with self-carriage and relaxation, showing no visible aids from the rider.

In classical horsemanship, the focus is on something that bears repeating: Anyone who trains and rides horses should treat them with care and consideration. This includes taking time and remaining calm, as well as understanding the differences between individual horses.

A horse should also have the chance to move relaxed and supple under the rider, and be ridden with a light, soft hand.

It should be obvious, right?

> ### Summary
> # Classical Horsemanship
> ### The Army Riding Regulation, *H. Dv. 12* with Commentary
>
> The *Heeresdienstvorschrift* [*H.Dv. 12 with Commentary*] is a key foundation of classical riding theory. Among other things, it states that horses must always be trained with consideration for their individual needs. This is also emphasized in the *Ethical Principles* of the German Equestrian Federation (FN).
>
> ### With Calm and Time
> Horse training must not happen under time pressure, or horses will become stressed and unwell.
>
> ### Relaxation (*Losgelassenheit*)
> Young horses first need to learn to move relaxed under the rider. They must practice how to carry the rider's weight in balance.
>
> ### The Rider's Aids
> Rein aids are used only for communication between horse and rider. There is no place for force or violence.

Chapter 3
Your Horse's Living Conditions
How Horses Want to Live

If you want to ride, you should know as much as possible about horses. You'll be able to understand them better if you know how horses behave and how they want to live.

In a social group, horses learn a lot. They must adapt to a hierarchy that reflects life in a natural herd.

The Horse as a Flight Animal

Horses are herd animals. Their original habitat was the open steppe[1]. There, they spent the entire day searching for food and moving around. Throughout, they remained highly alert—because horses are prey animals. That means when faced with danger, they prefer to flee rather than fight. Horses defend themselves only in emergencies, when there is no other option.

As flight animals, horses rely on excellent all-around vision. They must be able to detect predators in time to escape quickly.

Because of the side placement of their eyes, horses can see almost everything around them—except what is directly in front of their nose

---

[1] A steppe is an ecoregion characterized by grassland plains without closed forests except near rivers and lakes. The term steppe climate denotes a semi-arid climate, which is encountered in regions too dry to support a forest, but not dry enough to be a desert. - Wikipedia - Editor's note.

or right behind them. To see those areas, they must turn their head. How sharply a horse sees something depends on distance. That's why horses sometimes shy away from objects directly in front of them—they're trying to get a better look. But horses also have other highly developed senses. They can smell much better than humans, almost as well as dogs. They also have excellent hearing. Horses react to voices and sounds much sooner than we do. Even when dozing or eating, they immediately notice interesting noises. The ear muscles are always directed toward the source of the sound—whether it's in front of, beside, or behind the horse. The horse will then turn its ears, its head, or even its entire body in that direction.

Once you realize that a flight animal like the horse is always alert and constantly observing its surroundings, it becomes clear just how difficult it can be for a horse to concentrate on its rider. And when a horse gets startled, it will try to flee—that's something we as humans must always be prepared for.

The Connemara stallion shown here is allowed to express his joy of movement for at least 6 hours every day.

Not like this! But like this:

Cribbers, out of boredom, place their upper jaw and front teeth on objects like stall bars to gulp in air.

How Horses Should Live

You already know that horses are herd animals. But what does that mean for their life with us humans?

Horses always need the companionship of other horses. They become lonely and insecure without horse friends. You can be a friend to your horse too, but you can never replace other horses.

Horses need horse friends—and lots of space. A small stall is not enough—they're not standing animals, but moving and flight animals! Their entire body is designed for movement. In their original habitat, the steppe, they spent about 18 hours a day searching for food—which means they roamed around grazing rather than standing still. So if a horse spends 23 hours a day in a closed stall and only goes out for an hour of riding, it will get sick!

The whole body of a horse is geared toward constant foraging. Even the digestive system needs regular "refills"—that is, something to digest all the time. Large amounts of concentrated feed, like muesli or grain, stress the stomach and intestines and provide a sudden surge of energy. What horses really need is a steady supply of energy, which they get from hay or grass—not an occasional energy burst from a feed bucket. To stay healthy, they need lots of hay and grass—ideally enough so they have something to nibble on throughout the entire day.

Mutual grooming is a sign of friendship—almost like cuddling for horses!

In every herd, there is a hierarchy. You should always be the leader for your horse..

THREE THINGS YOUR HORSE NEEDS:

- Horses need other horses
- Horses need space
- Horses need plenty of roughage, such as hay, straw, and grass

Here you see dominance fights and rough play in two phases—a normal part of daily life for horses on pasture.

RESPONSIBILITY

You should always give your horse enough freedom to express its natural instincts.

Anyone who rides takes on responsibility for the horse—the responsibility to ensure that the horse is kept and ridden in a way that causes no harm. This applies especially to those who train horses.

Summary
Your Horse's Living Conditions

The Horse as a Flight Animal
Horses need movement throughout the entire day. They are highly alert, and their senses—sight, smell, and hearing—are very well developed.

How Horses Should Live
Horses need companionship with other horses, plenty of space, and lots of roughage.

Responsibility
If you ride a horse, you must also ensure it is living in a species-appropriate way.

Every rider is responsible for keeping your horse in a species-appropriate way and riding it with sensitivity—for your horse's sake!

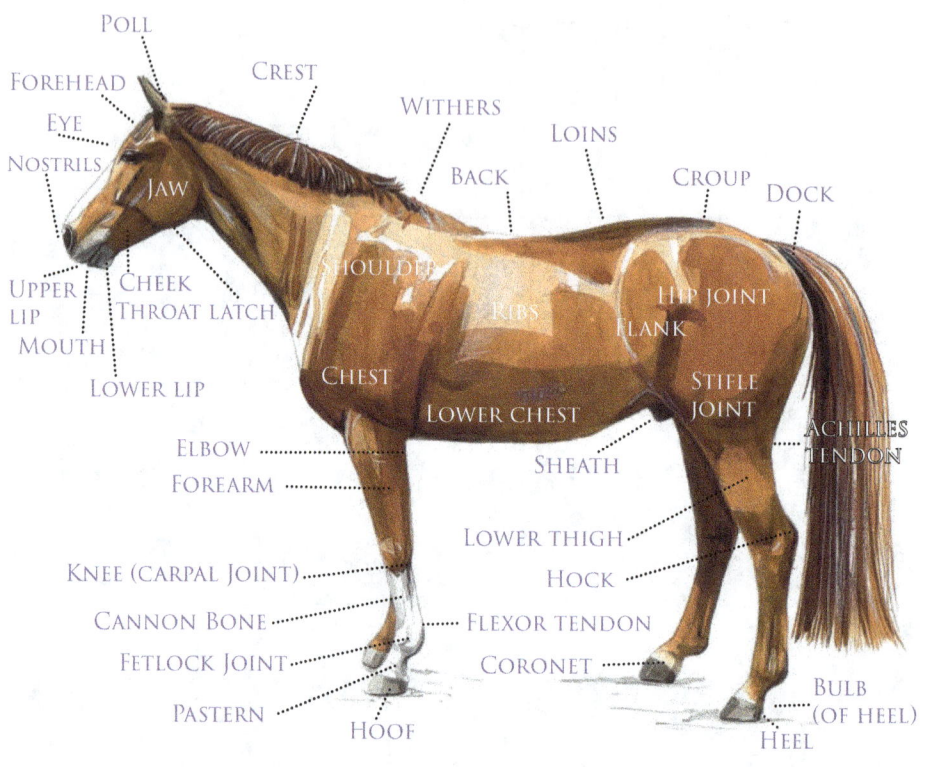

Chapter 4

The Horse's Body

The Anatomy of Your Horse

A typical warmblood horse weighs about 550 to 650 kg (1,200–1,430 lbs.), while a riding pony weighs around 400 to 450 kg (880–990 lbs.) 600 kg—that's roughly the weight of eight adult men—so it's really quite a lot! When a rider is on a horse, they put pressure on the horse's back and shift its balance.

The Bridge Construction

Most of the horse's weight is essentially suspended between the front and hind legs, mainly in the abdominal area, which is supported by the spine. The thoracic and lumbar vertebrae form a bridge between the shoulder blades and the pelvis.

THE HEAD

The head is connected to the cervical spine. At the occipital bone, the nuchal ligament begins—one of the most important ligaments in the horse's bridge-like body structure.

THE CERVICAL SPINE

At the poll, the cervical spine connects to the head. It consists of seven vertebrae that, together, form an S-shaped structure. It is, along with the tail, the most flexible part of the spine and plays a crucial role in the horse's balance.

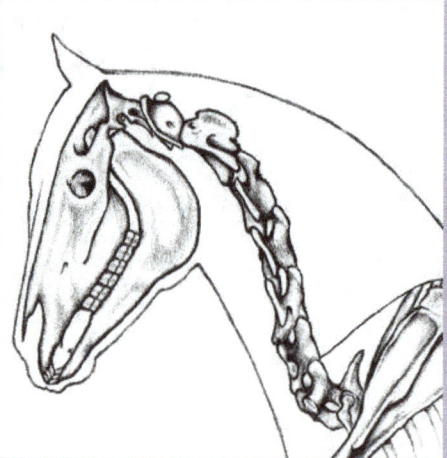

The cervical spine runs in the shape of an "S."

The Thoracic Spine

The thoracic spine consists of 18 vertebrae, which are relatively short and less flexible than the cervical vertebrae. A special feature of the thoracic spine is the presence of very long spinous processes.

The spinous processes of the 2nd to 10th thoracic vertebrae form the withers. These are significantly longer than those of the other vertebrae.

The ribs are attached to the 18 thoracic vertebrae. The front eight ribs are connected directly to the sternum, while the rear ten ribs have cartilage ends that form what's called the costal arch. These are attached flexibly, allowing the horse to breathe freely.

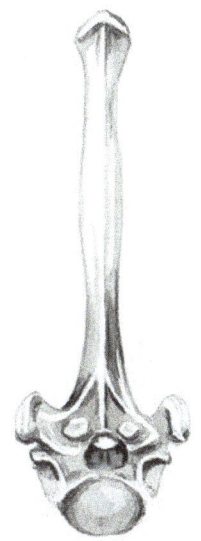

Thoracic vertebra from the withers area with long spinous processes.

The Thoracic Vertebra

Thoracic vertebrae have very long spinous processes—up to 30 cm long. These processes can come into contact with each other in the thoracic and lumbar spine region, potentially causing a condition known as "Kissing Spine Syndrome." Horses affected by this condition may suffer from severe back pain.

The Lumbar Vertebra

The six lumbar vertebrae are located directly behind the thoracic spine. They have long lateral transverse processes and rather short spinous processes. This is where the strongest part of the long back muscle is located. If the horse is well-muscled, this muscle helps stabilize the lumbar spine.

Lumbar vertebra with long transverse processes and rather short spinous processes.

The Sacrum

The sacrum consists of five fused vertebrae. It connects to the pelvis at the sacroiliac joint. This is a very important joint because it is where all the power from the horse's hind legs is transferred to the spine.

Tail (Coccygeal) Vertebrae

The tail vertebrae consist of 18 to 21 vertebrae. A horse's tail carriage is a clear indicator of its level of relaxation and comfort. A tense horse that feels uncomfortable will swish or flick its tail nervously. In contrast, a relaxed and supple horse will allow its tail to swing loosely in rhythm with its movement.

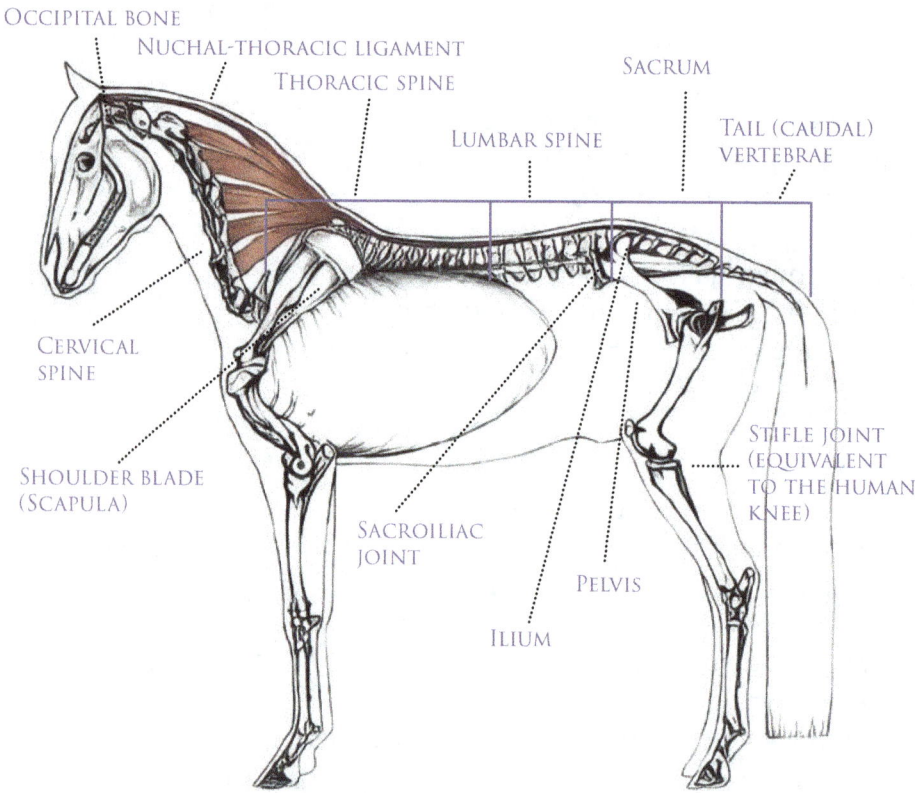

LIGAMENTS

Ligaments support the horse's body. They connect bones to joints and provide stability. The spine features several long ligaments, the most important being the nuchal ligament and the supraspinous (back) ligament. These are the main components of what is known as the "upper tension system"—the structure that runs from the horse's head to the sacrum.

The Nuchal Ligament

The nuchal ligament is a 4 to 5 cm wide tendinous band. It extends from the head to the thoracic spine, ending at the withers. At the withers, it is attached to the spinous processes, and the point of attachment is known as the withers cap (*Widerristkappe*). From this cap, the second part of the ligament fans forward to connect with the cervical spine

A very tense horse.

The Supraspinous (Back) Ligament

The supraspinous ligament runs from the withers cap to the sacrum. It connects all the spinous processes of the back and ends in fibers at the sacrum.

MUSCLES

A horse has approximately 504 muscles and 205 bones. The long muscles are responsible for movement, while the short muscles support the skeleton and are responsible for coordination.

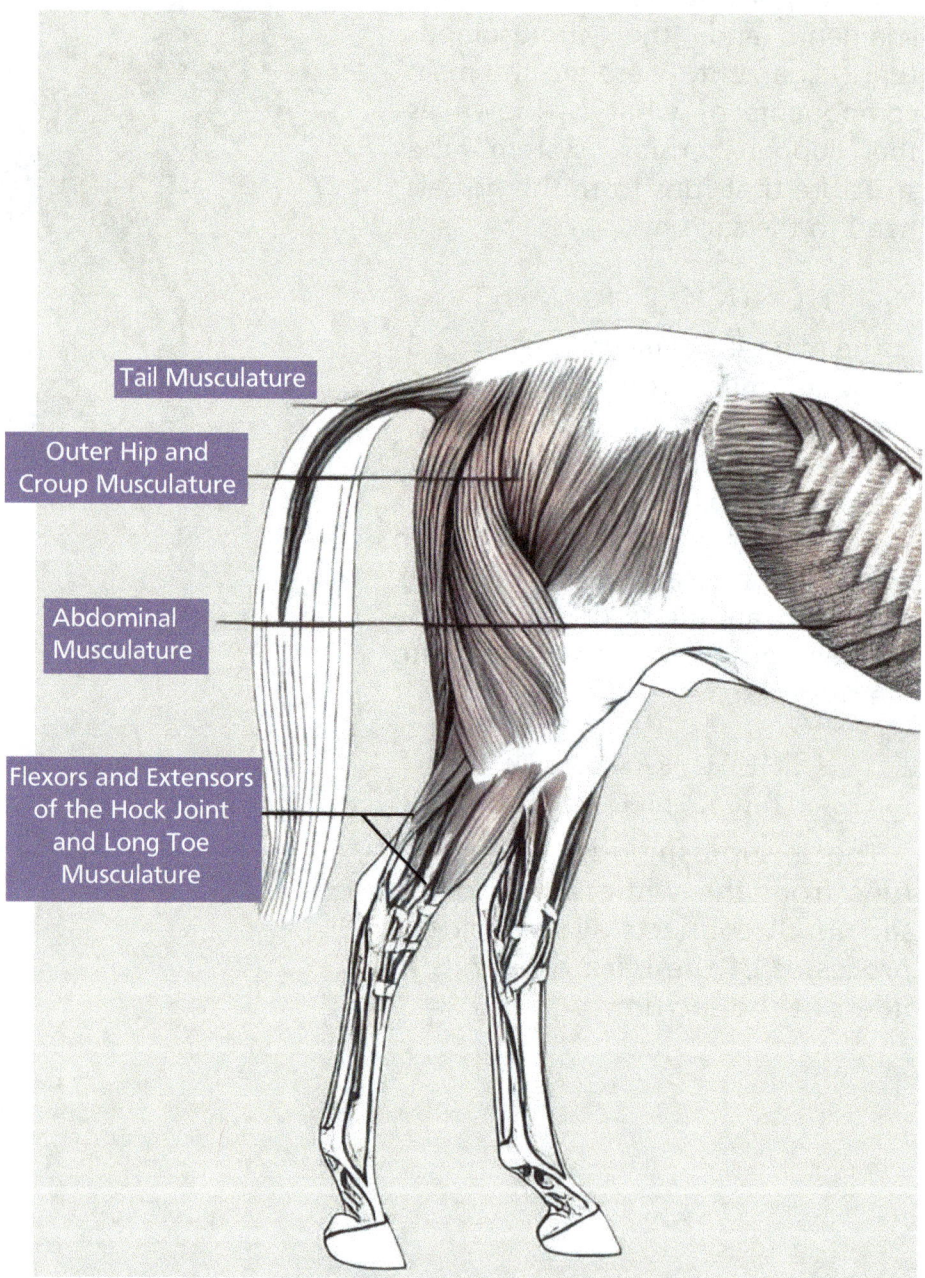

The muscles provide stability to the entire body by maintaining a basic level of tension. The contracting and relaxing of muscles is what creates movement. Muscles are connected to bones via tendons, and in this way, muscles are essentially responsible for the mobility of the horse's body.

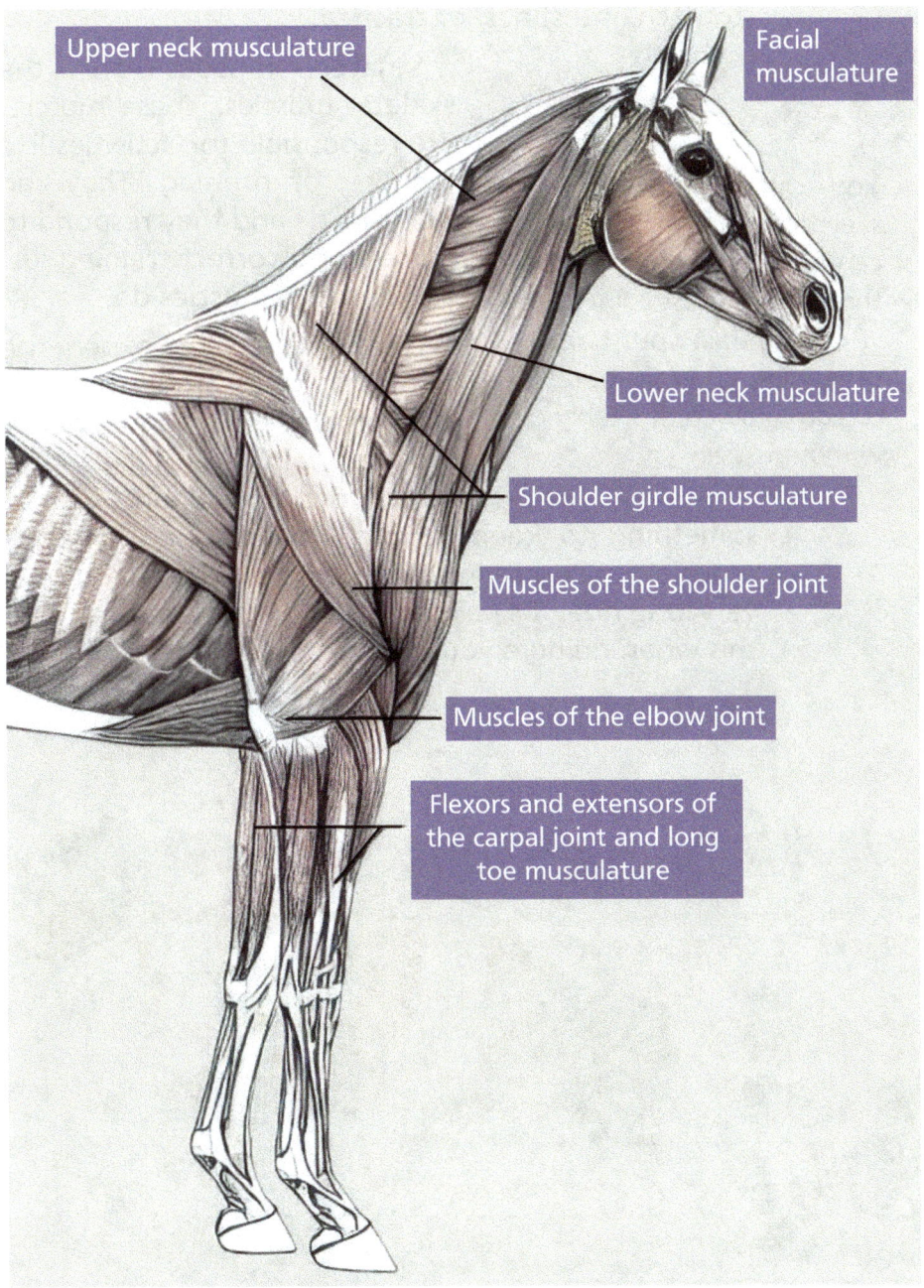

Skeletal Muscles

A horse's muscle system consists of smooth, striated (skeletal), and cardiac muscle.

Smooth muscle is controlled by the autonomic nervous system and cannot be consciously controlled. This includes muscles found in areas such as the stomach, intestines, or trachea.

Muscles

You can train a horse's skeletal muscles just like you can build your own muscles through exercise. In fact, you must train your horse—otherwise, it won't be able to carry you comfortably or without issues!

Striated muscles are the skeletal muscles. These muscles are responsible for activities like jumping or running. They can be trained—and they respond to correct or incorrect training just like our own muscles do.

Horses can also experience muscle soreness from training. Unfamiliar exertion causes muscle pain in horses just as it does in humans. This is something to keep in mind when riding a horse, especially when trying something new or going on a very long ride. It's particularly important to remember this when riding a young horse!

THE LONG BACK MUSCLE

The long back muscle is responsible for lateral bending and stretching of the neck and back when the horse is standing. When the horse is moving, this muscle plays a key role in movement and the quality of the natural gaits. Despite appearances, this muscle is not meant for carrying weight. The muscle fibers that make up the long back muscle are not suited for bearing loads.

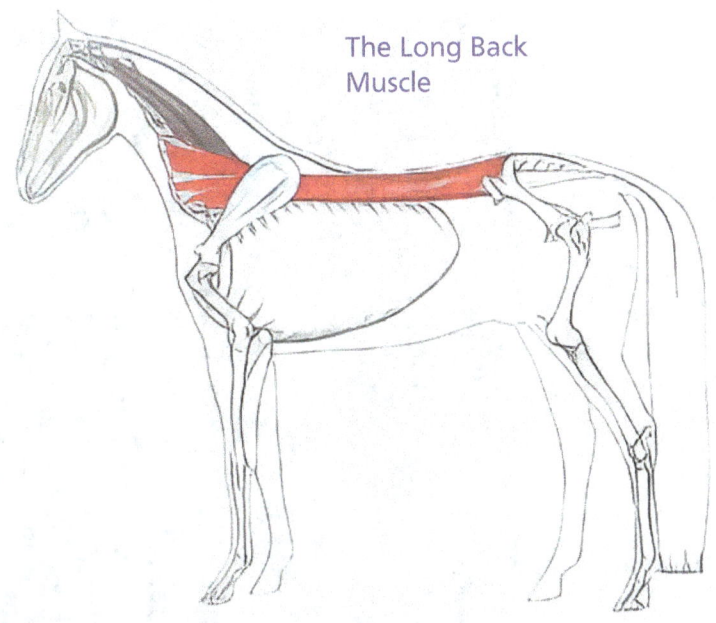

The Long Back Muscle

The long back muscle allows the horse to lift its trunk. A good example of this muscle being used is in the Levade. During every canter stride, trot step, or walking movement, this muscle helps raise the trunk. In the natural basic gaits, the long back muscle lifts the trunk from behind, that is, when the horse's hind legs are in contact with the ground—working from the rear base of support. When a horse is playing and jumping around energetically, the action base of the long back muscle shifts to the front, and the hindquarters may lift off, for example, in a playful buck.

An exemplary Levade. The long back muscles lift the trunk.

The Horse's Back

The long back muscle plays a crucial role in determining whether a horse moves with a tense, loose, or engaged (carrying) back. And depending on how supple the back is, the rider will find it easier or harder to sit comfortably on the horse.

> ## Facts
> ### Uncomfortable Ride?
> Horses that are difficult to sit on are often very tense. Their backs don't swing, and as a result, it's nearly impossible to sit the trot on these horses.

This horse moves with an engaged back and light, elastic contact. This rider should be wearing a helmet.

A pony moving in natural balance on a loose rein. The back muscles show little positive tension—the pony has not yet achieved true suppleness.

1. The Loose Back

A "loose" back refers to a horse's back that is neither positively engaged nor tense. Horses trained according to the original French school, sometimes move with a loose back. In such horses, rein contact is also minimal and inconsistent.

Horses trained according to the German Equestrian Federation's (FN) Guidelines for Riding and Driving are taught to maintain a light but steady connection with the bit, and great value is placed on a soft yet consistent contact. For a relaxed recreational or trail horse, this kind of natural balance can be sufficient, as long as the horse's body remains free of tension. Even a horse used purely for leisure or trail riding should have a basic level of suppleness, to avoid harming its body over time.

Beautiful, collected canter with a well-seated rider.

2. The Engaged (Carrying) Back

The engaged back—the goal of our training philosophy—emerges when the horse is so well balanced that it seeks contact with the bit, chewing softly and with a supple poll. A horse in this state carries its rider with positively engaged muscles, without straining its ligaments and supporting structures. The movements remain natural and pure. This is called the balanced state. The horse is in equilibrium. Its movements become more dynamic and expressive, even dance-like. With increasing positive tension in the back, more expression is visible in the natural gaits.

CAUTION!
Don't confuse this with mechanical, flashy movements like exaggeratedly suspended steps that are produced from a contracted and tense back (see photo on page 68, left side).

3. The Tense Back

Horses with a tight or stiff back often either hollow their back downward or overarch it, making it difficult for them to bring their hind legs properly under the body mass toward the center of gravity. Some horses, whose heads are forced downward, move with an excessively raised and tense back that is over-stretched rather than engaged.

The reason horses move with a tense back is, in most cases, the rider—either pulling too hard on the reins or sitting poorly and tensely—and often both. Such a horse can no longer be ridden comfortably. Over time, these horses often develop movement issues and health problems in the back and legs. These horses frequently show tense, floating steps, which might look impressive to the uneducated observer, but these false moving steps harm the horse! Judges should always give very low scores for this!

LOWER TENSION (*UNTERE VERSPANNUNG*)

The back is not only supported by the muscles along the top, but also "supported from below." The midline of the belly (where the straight abdominal muscles meet) is formed by a tendinous band (the white line). It connects the sternum to the pelvic arch (pubic bone) and passively stabilizes the trunk from below. However, the abdominal muscles do not have a true weight-bearing function. They are movement muscles and act like a hammock for the abdominal organs.

While the horse is cantering, the abdominal muscles contract during the suspension phase. This pulls the pelvis and hind legs forward, rounding the horse's frame. The abdominal muscles must move so that the horse can move. They cannot support the rider's weight or stabilize the back—because muscles that hold something must be tense, whereas the abdominal muscles are actively in motion.

Early practice makes a good rider. Here, a bit of balance is still missing...

Still: My favorite picture!

The Neck Musculature

When a horse has a well-shaped neck, we usually find it beautiful. But what exactly is a beautiful neck? A horse is said to have a beautiful neck when the top-line muscles (upper neck musculature) are well developed.

When the horse moves in a stretching posture (*Dehnungshaltung*), the upper neck muscles—together with the nuchal ligament, which acts passively—pull the spinous processes of the withers forward. The under neck muscles pull the head downward and bend the neck to the side. They also help in moving the front legs. However, they are not significantly developed during proper riding. In poorly ridden horses, especially those with incorrectly used training aids (such as draw reins), the horse may be forced to hold its head down, and tense upper neck muscles resist against this.

Over time, the under neck muscles become stronger, leading to incorrect muscling.

Well-shaped neck of a young horse.

This horse's neck is very short, and the jowls are very tight. The horse likely has difficulty maintaining proper contact with the bit (*Anlehnung*) [elastic support].

Medium-length neck with a good poll and moderately developed upper neck musculature.

The cervical spine [along with the tail] is the most flexible part of the horse's spine and plays a crucial role in the horse's balance. When a horse lowers its neck forward and downward, or carries it in a relative upright position, the nuchal ligament and supraspinous ligament can support the back in a relaxed, tension-free posture. This is the prerequisite for riding a horse without causing health problems. Only then can the back muscles work without tension.

The appearance of a horse's neck musculature also reveals whether it is being correctly ridden. A well-ridden horse has a nicely developed top-line (upper neck musculature) and little under neck development. If the opposite is true, there is usually something wrong with the horse's training or education.

Of course, there are individual differences: A Norwegian Fjord, for example, naturally has a shorter neck than a warmblood. It might be a bit harder for such a horse to let its neck stretch freely—but it can still learn! One horse may find this easier than another, but ultimately, every horse can and must be ridden correctly—otherwise, it will become ill.

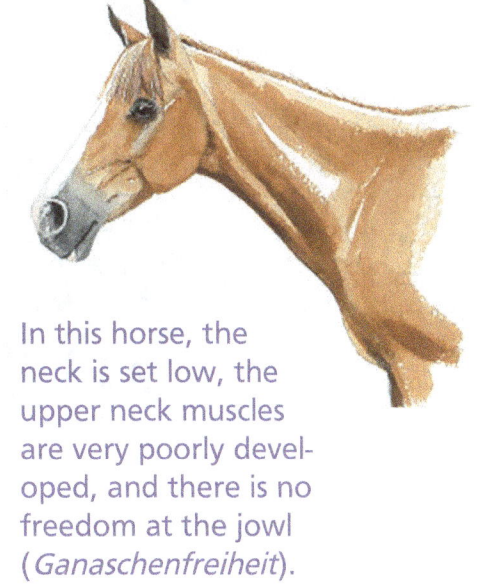

In this horse, the neck is set low, the upper neck muscles are very poorly developed, and there is no freedom at the jowl (*Ganaschenfreiheit*).

Here you can see the muscle layers in the horse's neck. In the first image, the deepest muscle is shown. The muscles in Image 2 lie above it.

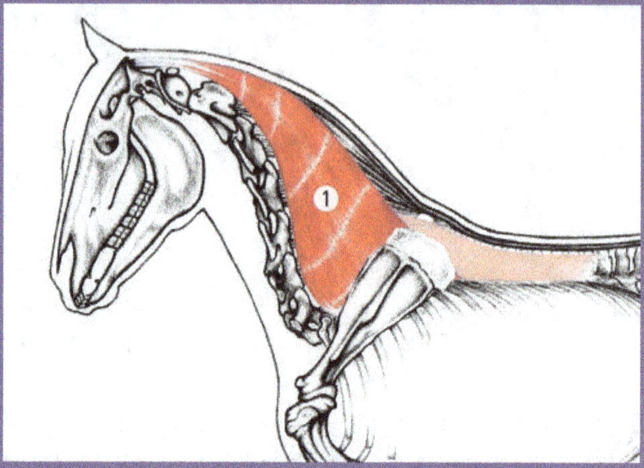

1 - Semispinalis capitis muscle — Image 1

The upper neck muscles shown here normally serve to move the neck and head. In classical riding theory, they are also attributed a back-supporting function. The neck acts as a lever arm and, through the spinous processes of the withers, creates a lifting effect on the back.

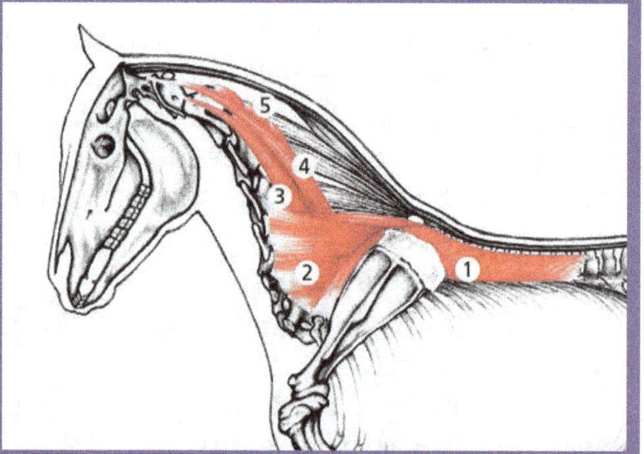

1 - Longissimus dorsi muscle — Image 2
2 - Longissimus cervicis muscle
3 - Longissimus atlantis muscle
4 - Longissimus capitis muscle
5 - Multifidus cervicis muscle

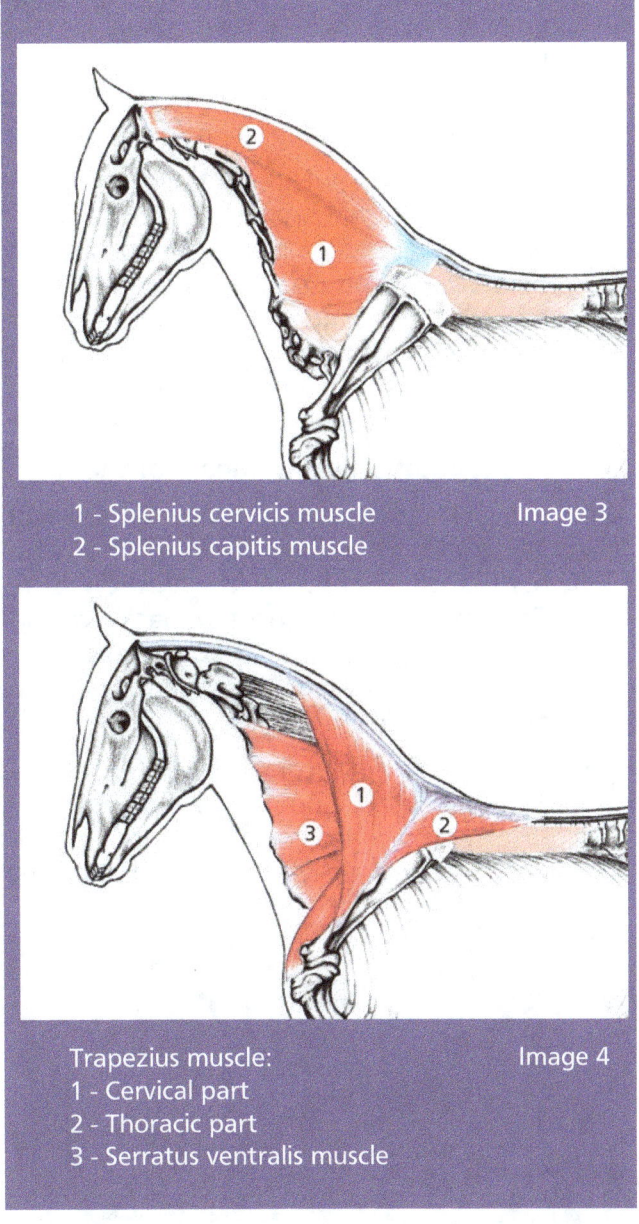

1 - Splenius cervicis muscle   Image 3
2 - Splenius capitis muscle

Trapezius muscle: Image 4
1 - Cervical part
2 - Thoracic part
3 - Serratus ventralis muscle

The muscles shown in Image 3 lie on top of those in Image 2. You can only feel the outermost muscle layer, which is shown in Image 4.

These muscles are capable of pulling the spinous processes of the withers forward and tensing the back ligament. In doing so, they lift the back. From this, you can understand how important it is to never (!) shorten a horse's neck by pulling on the reins. A well-developed top-line (upper neck) clearly indicates that a horse has been worked correctly.

The Croup and the Hindquarters

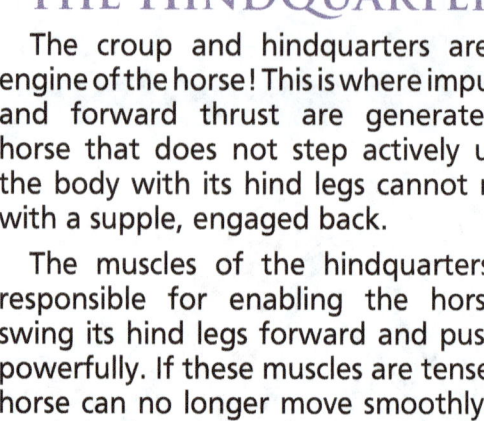

Well-shaped performance croup.

The stifle joint could be positioned further underneath the body. The croup is a bit too short (see page 44).

The croup and hindquarters are the engine of the horse! This is where impulsion and forward thrust are generated. A horse that does not step actively under the body with its hind legs cannot move with a supple, engaged back.

The muscles of the hindquarters are responsible for enabling the horse to swing its hind legs forward and push off powerfully. If these muscles are tense, the horse can no longer move smoothly. The result is choppy or shortened steps and strides. Often, the root cause of these shortened or tense strides is a tense back.

But what does this mean for the rider?

It means you must ensure that your horse moves actively forward and is not restricted by too much rein pressure. Otherwise, the horse's back cannot swing properly either. So always make sure that your horse's hind legs are active and engaged!

In the training scale, this is referred to as "rhythm" (*Takt*). But be careful—not every fast tempo is correct. It's important to find the correct rhythm for each individual horse, in order to move in balance.

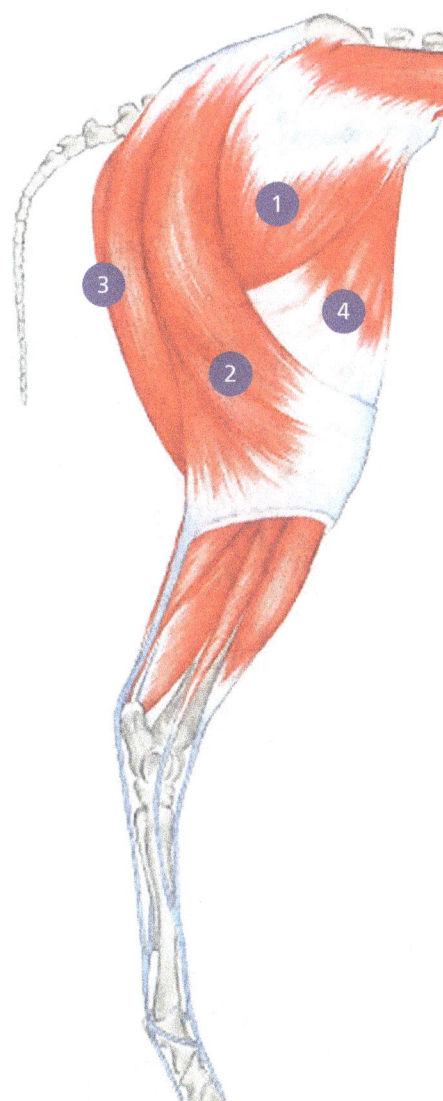

The large muscles of the croup and thigh function as either flexors or extensors of the associated joints, depending on the phase of movement (push-off, suspension, or stance phase).

1. The croup muscle (*Musculus glutaeus*) flexes and extends the hip joint. It has two distinct muscle bellies and is directly connected to the back.

2. The two-headed thigh muscle (*Musculus biceps femoris*) extends the hip, stifle, and hock joints, flexes the stifle, and moves the hind limb outward.

3. The semitendinosus muscle (*Musculus semitendinosus*) extends the hip and hock joint, while the semimembranosus muscle (*Musculus semimembranosus*) also extends the hip and draws the limb inward.

4. The four-headed thigh muscle (*Musculus quadriceps femoris*) flexes the hip, extends the stifle, and stabilizes it.

In the wild, horses graze for an average of 18 hours per day.

The Horse's Body and What Happens During Riding

Natural Posture

Grazing is the most natural posture for a horse: the head and neck are stretched downward and forward. In this position, wild horses spend 17 to 19 hours a day searching for food. The horse's body is therefore designed to graze for long periods without any difficulty. But what happens when we ride?

This grey horse moves in an exemplary stretching frame; every horse should develop this willingness to stretch.

A horse with a long upper neckline can carry both the rider's weight and the weight of its own trunk without difficulty. For this reason, young horses and horses in the loosening (warm-up) phase should be ridden forward-downward. This posture is called the stretching frame (*Dehnungshaltung*).

Relaxed rising trot on a long rein.

Young horses, in particular, do not yet have sufficient muscle strength to carry the rider with an upright neck. When they are ridden in a natural posture, it is much easier for them to balance their body with the rider's weight.

A horse ridden forward and downward (*vorwärts-abwärts*) can thus remain in balance, allowing its back to swing freely and relaxed. Only then can a horse move naturally in all three gaits and step actively under with its hindquarters. Even an older and more advanced horse should never lose its willingness to stretch. A supple back is the prerequisite for the rider to sit without tension and to maintain soft, sensitive contact.

The Stretching Frame (*Dehnungshaltung*)

A horse ridden in a stretching frame can carry the rider's weight without straining or trying to support the additional load using the long back muscle.

A content horse in a stretching posture without saddle or bridle. You should never copy this—always wear a helmet!

This three-year-old Fjord gelding is just beginning his training under saddle. We wish him a rider who is kind and understanding!

It can step forward actively from behind, using its hind legs in a way that allows impulsion to flow from back to front through the entire body—all the way to the rider's soft hands.

Young horses need about one to two years before they are strong enough to carry the rider's weight in a more upright head-neck posture, known as "relative elevation." This posture is not an end in itself. A young horse needs the stretching frame to find its balance under the rider's weight. An older, more advanced horse can also relax in the stretching frame, but the willingness to stretch must always be present and accessible at any time.

THE ABILITIES OF YOUNG HORSES AT A GLANCE

1. Young horses should not be ridden continuously for more than 10 minutes. After that, they get tired and raise their heads.
2. In that moment, you should never continue riding and try to force their head or neck into the "correct" position. Instead, the horse needs a short break of about 5 minutes with a loose rein.
3. Horses are not disobedient on purpose—there is usually a reason why they resist a certain exercise. Often, the resistance is caused by muscle pain.

THE BASIC GAITS

The so-called basic gaits of the horse include three movements: walk, trot, and canter.

THE WALK

The walk is the slowest gait and is a four-beat gait. First, the right hind leg steps down, followed by the right front leg, then the left hind leg, and finally the left front leg.

The neck performs a rhythmic nodding and swinging motion. This is because the long back muscle alternately contracts and relaxes with each step. If this nodding movement of the head and neck is restricted by the rider's hands, the horse's back becomes tense, and the horse can no longer walk with a clear, relaxed rhythm.

In the walk, the two legs on the same side (right or left) form a "V" shape.

THE TROT

The trot is a two-beat gait with a moment of suspension in between—a phase where none of the horse's hooves touch the ground. In the trot, the horse moves its diagonal pairs of legs simultaneously—that is, the right front and left hind move together, and the left front and right hind move together. Because of the suspension phase, the trot can feel a bit bouncy for the rider. If the horse's back is tense, its hind legs can no longer swing forward properly in the trot. It can look almost as if the hind legs don't belong to the horse's body. In some incorrect "showy" riding styles, often seen in competition, this kind of incorrect movement is common and mistakenly awarded high scores, simply because the front legs are flung forward in an exaggerated "eye-catching" manner.

In the trot, you can clearly see the diagonal leg pairs moving forward together. The young lady should be wearing a helmet.

The Canter

The canter is a three-beat gait with a jumping, bounding motion. There are two types: left lead and right lead. In left lead canter, the horse pushes further under its body with the left hind leg; in right lead canter, it pushes more with the right hind leg. The inside front leg reaches farther forward in each case.

The six phases of the canter, as shown in the illustration above, are:

1. Single-leg support (outside hind leg)
2. Three-leg support (outside hind leg from phase 1, inside hind leg, outside front leg)
3. Two-leg support (inside hind leg, outside front leg)
4. Three-leg support (inside hind leg, outside front leg, inside front leg)
5. Single-leg support (inside front leg)
6. Suspension phase

To truly canter in a three-beat rhythm, the horse's back muscles must be supple.

Shown here is a right-lead canter. The young lady should be wearing a helmet.

Problems Caused by the Rider

When a horse is over-flexed by reins that pull backward too strongly, the long back muscle becomes tense. This leads, for example, to the horse's walk turning into a pacing gait—that is, the normal four-beat walk shifts into a two-beat rhythm. The front and hind legs on the same side move at the same time. The horse moves like a camel—this is called pacing.

If a horse is ridden like this for an extended period, the long back muscle becomes stiff and hard, and the horse develops back pain. Many cases of lameness originate from this kind of tense, mechanical riding! Horses ridden under such forced conditions often end up needing corrective training or become chronically unsound. This kind of riding is usually accompanied by a harsh hand and a stiff, pushing seat (known as a *Schiebesitz*) [Sliding seat]. Learn the light seat!

Even in the trot, movement is affected by rough rein use and a tense seat. The horse may throw its front legs forward in a flashy way, but the hind legs fail to engage properly. Oskar Maria Stensbeck, in his 1931 book *Reiten*, called this the so-called "show trot" or "competition trot." Unfortunately, this kind of movement is still often seen in dressage competitions.

Purity of Gaits

In a well-ridden horse, the natural footfall sequence is never disrupted by the rider. The incorrect, tense so-called "show trot" or "competition trot" is so harmful to horses that it can lead to leg problems and back pain. Many horses cannot sustain these flashy steps for long and their bodies wear out very quickly.

The Head-Neck Axis

When a horse is ridden with a long neck and nose at the vertical, its back can swing freely and without tension.

Thus, we distinguish between three types of posture:

1. The natural posture with an engaged back (stretching frame, relative elevation → back mover) [Correct]
2. The high, overly tight posture with a hollow back (absolute elevation → leg mover) [Incorrect]
3. The tight, overly deep posture with a tense, over-bent back (rollkur, hyper-flexion → tense back mover) [Incorrect]

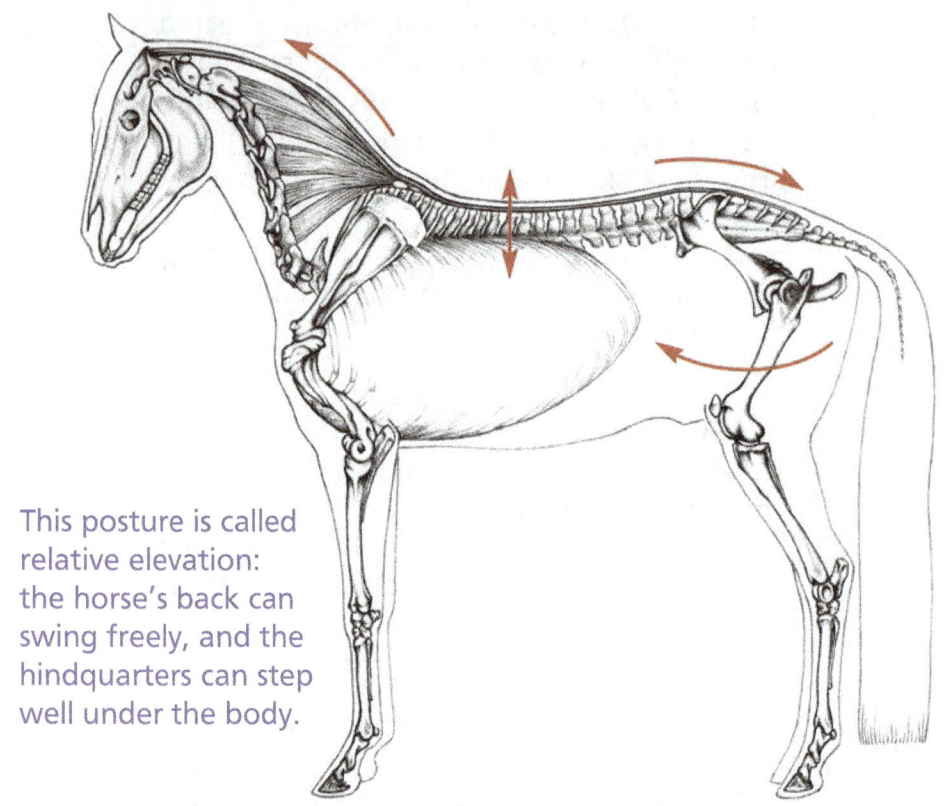

This posture is called relative elevation: the horse's back can swing freely, and the hindquarters can step well under the body.

The Natural Posture with an Engaged Back (Back Mover)

A horse moving in this posture is relaxed and rhythmically correct; its back is soft, supple, and free of tension. After one and a half to two years under saddle, a horse in good balance can begin to achieve the first mild degrees of collection. It becomes able to carry more weight with the hind legs and shift its center of gravity toward the haunches.

No matter whether the horse is used for dressage, jumping, or trail riding, it can only stay healthy if it moves in natural balance. And only if it is healthy can it remain capable, calm, and emotionally balanced.

Horses on a Loose Rein

Horses that are ridden on a rein that is too long and loose often move with less impulsion, and sometimes they even lose rhythm. However, this style of riding generally does not harm them.

The High and Tight Head-Neck Position with a Hollow Back (*Leg Mover*)

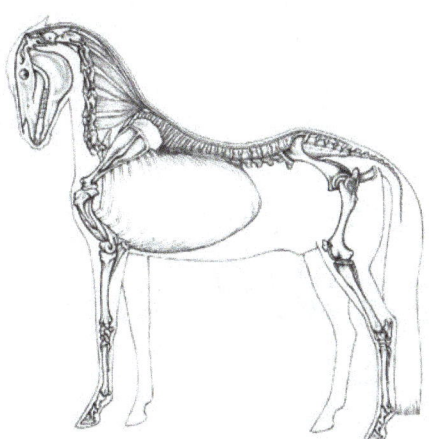

In this posture, the horse is ridden with heavy rein contact that forces the neck tighter and higher. The rider often sits with a tense, pushing seat, which blocks the horse's back. As a result, the horse's natural balance is lost. Horses ridden in this way often become unmotivated and tense. Some may even resist the rider, toss their heads, or buck. In addition, these horses often develop health issues, such as back pain and leg problems.

In mechanically over-flexed horses, the neck is too short, the back no longer engaged, and the hind legs cannot step under.

The Over-bent Posture with a Tense Back (*Tension Back Mover*)

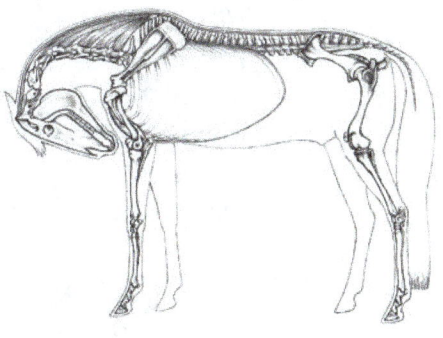

In this posture, the horse is also forced into an unnatural position. The horse's head is pulled down with the reins, causing the back to lift unnaturally and making it impossible for the back to move fluidly. When horses are ridden this way for an extended period, their back musculature changes, and their hindquarters can no longer step properly underneath the body. These horses often run away from the rider's weight, and the rider responds by pulling even harder on the reins in an attempt to slow them down.

The technical term for this is hyper-flexion or Rollkur. Horses subjected to this cruel treatment experience intense psychological and physical stress. Do not do this to your horse.

When the head is pulled to the chest, the horse's back is overstretched, and the hind legs trail out behind. This puts the horse in a state of extreme psychological stress.

Summary
The Anatomy of Your Horse

The Spine

- The thoracic and lumbar spine of the horse forms a bridge between the forehand and hindquarters.
- The cervical spine (neck) is the most mobile part of the spine.
- The thoracic vertebrae have very long spinous processes in the area of the withers.
- The strongest part of the long back muscle is attached to the lumbar spine, where it functions as a trunk lifter.
- The sacroiliac joint is extremely important: this is where the power from the hind legs is transferred into the spine.

The Ligaments

The most important parts of the upper tension system are the nuchal ligament and the supraspinous (back) ligament.

The Muscles

The long muscles provide movement, the short ones support the skeleton and are responsible for coordination.

The long back muscle is responsible for the lateral bending and stretching of the neck and back. It is not there to carry weight. As a lifter of the trunk, it is one of the strongest movement muscles in the horse's body.

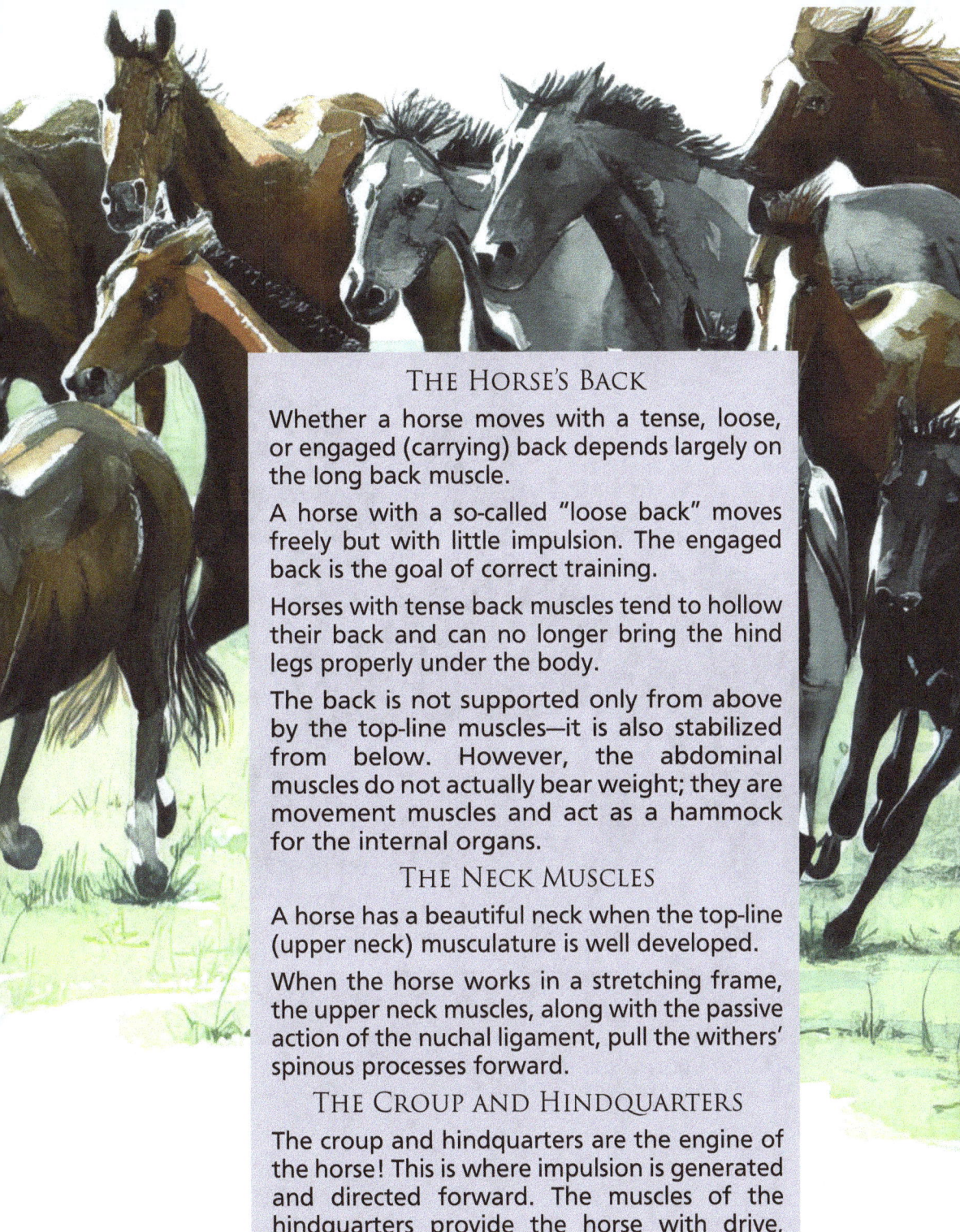

The Horse's Back

Whether a horse moves with a tense, loose, or engaged (carrying) back depends largely on the long back muscle.

A horse with a so-called "loose back" moves freely but with little impulsion. The engaged back is the goal of correct training.

Horses with tense back muscles tend to hollow their back and can no longer bring the hind legs properly under the body.

The back is not supported only from above by the top-line muscles—it is also stabilized from below. However, the abdominal muscles do not actually bear weight; they are movement muscles and act as a hammock for the internal organs.

The Neck Muscles

A horse has a beautiful neck when the top-line (upper neck) musculature is well developed.

When the horse works in a stretching frame, the upper neck muscles, along with the passive action of the nuchal ligament, pull the withers' spinous processes forward.

The Croup and Hindquarters

The croup and hindquarters are the engine of the horse! This is where impulsion is generated and directed forward. The muscles of the hindquarters provide the horse with drive, jumping power, and carrying capacity.

Rider in exemplary balanced seat, horse in excellent posture in right-lead canter. Rider should be wearing a helmet.

Chapter 5

Training Horses with Calm and Patience

Training a horse takes time. Young horses first need to get used to people and learn to trust them. This starts with simple things like haltering and tying, as well as cleaning their hooves. All of this is new and unfamiliar for young horses, and it must be introduced to them calmly and patiently. The more carefully and thoroughly this trust-building phase is developed, the more smoothly the process of starting the young horse under saddle will go.

The Training Scale

The foundation of the German Equestrian Federation's (FN) training guidelines is the Training Scale. It defines the elements of horse training in a logical progression: Rhythm, Relaxation, Contact, Impulsion, Straightness, and Collection.

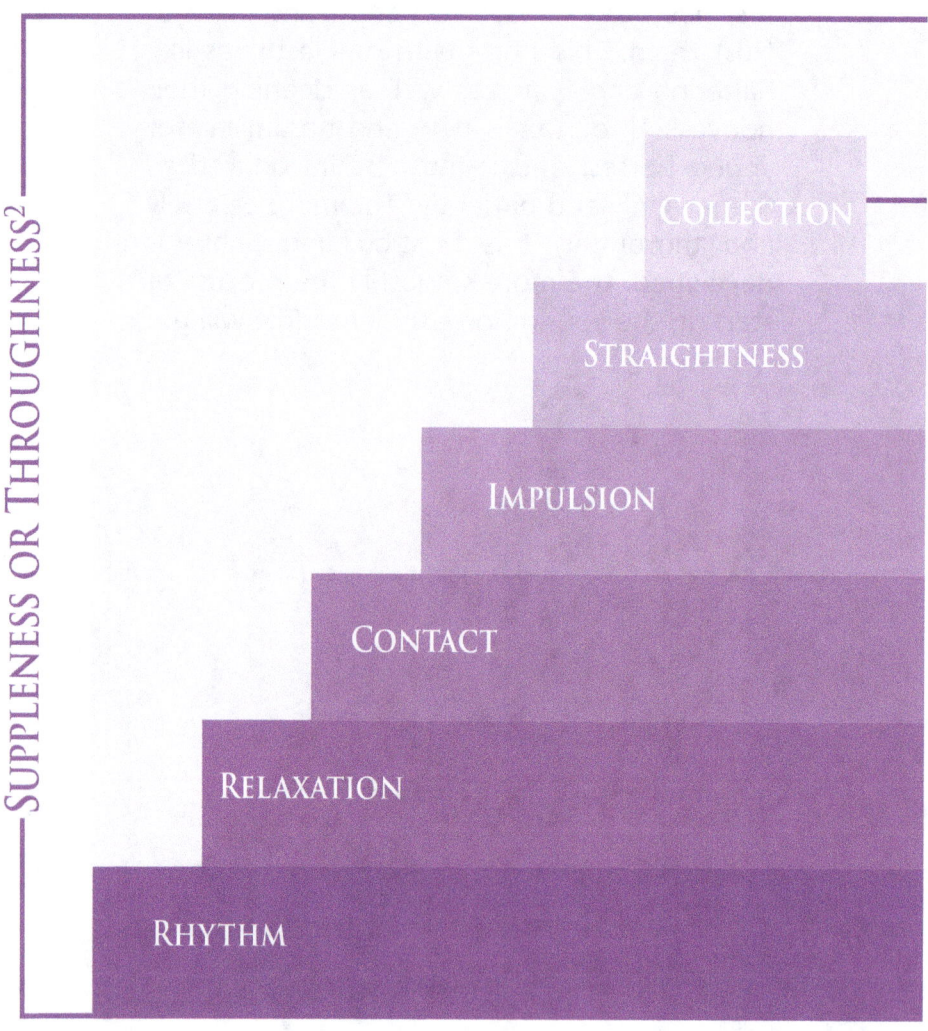

[2] In equestrian terms, Suppleness or Throughness refers to the horse's ability to respond willingly and softly to the rider's aids, with unrestricted flow of energy from back to front and front to back, and without resistance. A *"durchlässig"* horse is relaxed, attentive, and elastic, allowing the rider's aids to pass through the body without tension. - Editor's note.

A horse should learn to move in a clear and regular rhythm under the rider. All three basic gaits must remain pure in rhythm. Only then can a horse achieve relaxation. It should move with a soft contact, meaning a light, elastic connection to the rider's hand. In this way, the horse can gradually learn to move with impulsion and energy.

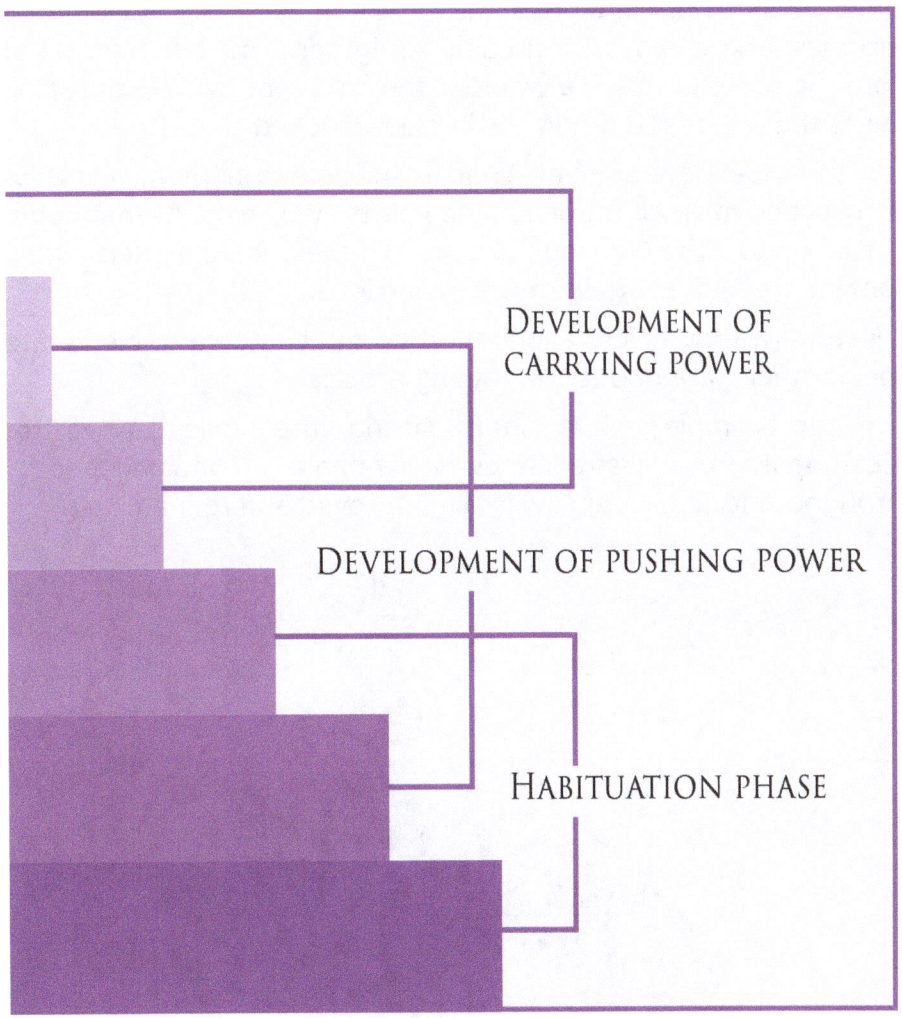

The Training Scale is not a static structure. Its individual components flow into one another and are mutually dependent. It serves as a very important guide in the training of our horses.[3]

---

[3] For a detailed explanation of how to understand and use the training scale in daily work and over the career of the horse and rider, refer to *The Elements of Dressage*, by Kurd Albrecht von Ziegner, ISBN: 9781948717489, Xenophon Press 2022. - Editor's note.

As training progresses, the horse is straightened. Every horse is naturally crooked from birth—similar to a person being right- or left-handed.

Through good training, horses become evenly supple in both directions and willing bend and position with equal facility. Even on curved lines, they learn to move with their hind legs stepping toward the center of gravity. The hindquarters begin to carry more weight.

The better a horse is trained, the more symmetrical its musculature becomes, and it moves noticeably straighter. You can even see it from the ground: observe whether the hind feet track in the same line as the front feet. If not, the horse is crooked.

With proper development, a horse can begin to learn the first steps of collection after about one and a half to two years. At that point, all elements of the Training Scale are achieved: Rhythm, Relaxation, Contact, Impulsion, Straightness, Collection.

Naturally, they follow a logical order and continue to blend into one another throughout the training process.

If, for example, relaxation is missing, the horse cannot trot with impulsion, and straightness will remain an ongoing priority throughout its life. It can always be improved and refined.

This is what harmony looks like when the foundational training is correct.

As the horse becomes increasingly relaxed and accepting of the aids, it also becomes more supple and responsive.

Throughness (*"Durchlässigkeit"*) [permeability] is the goal of all horse training, and is equally important for dressage and jumping horses as it is for pleasure horses. Throughness means that the horse or pony accepts the rider's aids without hesitation or resistance. Every horse needs a solid foundational training in order to carry humans without difficulty—regardless of whether it will one day compete in dressage, Western events, or simply be ridden through the woods.

Never attempt such exercises without a helmet! These girls are taking far too much risk.

It takes a long time to reach this kind of amazing freedom and connection with your horse. We are not speaking against saddle and bridle—quite the opposite! What we want to show you is this trust-based partnership, which should be the goal of every form of training, both in the saddle and on the ground.

Contact (*Anlehnung*)

Gentle on the back – the light seat.

Contact refers to the soft connection between the rider's hand and the horse's mouth via the reins. It is important that this connection is sensitive and consistent. Contact cannot be forced by pulling on the reins. Without the rider's seat and leg aids, there can be no correct contact.

And only when the horse's back can swing freely and elastically can the horse's mouth be relaxed enough to allow for a soft, accepting contact.

Facts

It cannot be said often enough:

Contact cannot be achieved by pulling on the reins. The horse must step forward freely from behind into the rider's hand. Anyone who pulls on the reins prevents the horse from lifting and engaging its back.

So, handle the reins with care!

A horse whose mouth is strapped shut with a noseband that is too tight will never be able to go in correct contact, because the animal is prevented from chewing. True contact is only possible with a mobile, relaxed mouth. Chewing is a must for every horse to achieve relaxation.

Contact always involves soft, careful rein handling. You must never try to force a horse into contact. Just as carefully as you ride a horse onto the bit, you must also adjust the bridle and noseband with care.

The noseband must not be fastened too tightly.

So always make sure your noseband is loose enough to give your horse room to move its lower jaw. You should be able to fit two upright fingers between the noseband and the nasal bone. The horse in the picture above is not wearing a flash strap, only a plain cavesson (English noseband). When fitted loosely, it allows the horse to chew and breathe properly.

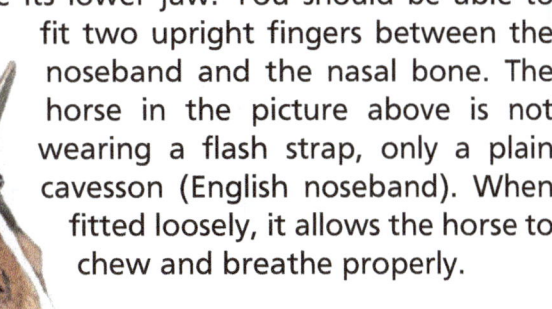

The dropped (Hanoverian) noseband must not sit so low that it interferes with breathing.

It quickly becomes clear how harmful a rough rein hand can be for the horse when you look again at its anatomy: The head and neck are connected at the top—at the poll. When you pull on the bit with force, strong pressure is applied to the poll and the attachment point of the nuchal ligament. This, in turn, causes tension in the horse's back. Your horse may become stiff, unwilling to move, resist your aids, or become dull and sluggish.

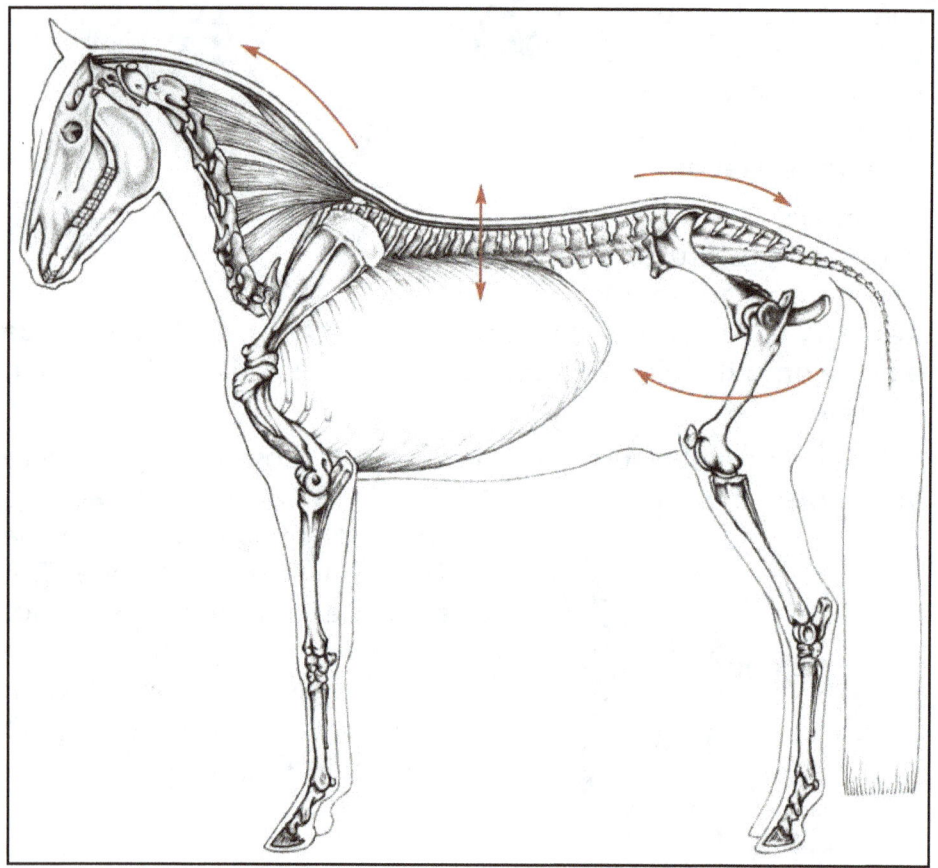

This is what correct self-carriage looks like: The horse's back is relaxed, and the hindquarters can step well underneath the body.

A horse is being ridden correctly when it moves in age-appropriate balance with supple musculature. If the rider also has a balanced seat, the horse can then step forward into the rider's sensitive hand. Contact is created by forward impulsion from the hindquarters—not by pulling from the front! The horse reaches for the hand, not the other way around.

In the image on the left, you can see a horse's body in relative self-carriage. The head is not pulled down, the neck is not forced low— on the contrary: the horse is standing in natural balance, the result of calm and sensitive training.

Contact cannot be forced. Training aids can help show the horse how to stretch its neck, but should never be used to force a head or neck position. Your instructor can show you how to properly use a martingale or triangle reins.

Draw reins, however, are extremely dangerous training aids. They exert excessive backward force and, if used incorrectly, can cause severe physical and emotional harm to horses. Best advice: NEVER use them! They double the power of your hands and create a shortened neck, which leads to a tight, tense back.

And you already know the consequences of that!

> ### FACTS
> DRAW REINS
> (*SCHLAUFZÜGEL*)
>
> Draw reins are completely unsuitable for riding. Strangely, there are still people who believe they can use them to ride a horse into contact. The opposite is true: **Draw reins harm the horse.**

Well-seated rider on a balanced horse at a free walk.

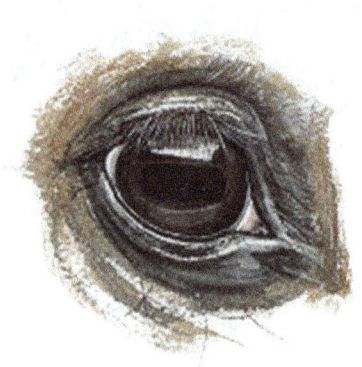

Young Horses

In the first one and a half years, young horses should primarily learn to carry the rider in balance. Rhythm, relaxation, and contact are the goals of this initial basic training.

Too much rein influence at this stage greatly harms the young horse's development. It first needs to build sufficient skeletal musculature before it can truly become a riding horse. Especially young horses should be allowed to move freely with a natural head and neck posture. They must first find their balance under the rider—balance and rhythm are not so easy for them. This basic training certainly doesn't take just a quick three weeks; depending on the horse, it can take up to two years. By the way, young horses learn best to move forward energetically when out on a hack. But even for older horses, a trail ride is excellent training! Plus, such rides are a lot of fun and expose young horses to many new experiences that they will encounter again later. After all, a horse shouldn't jump into the ditch every time it sees a tractor!

Riding out is not just fun for the horses!

Impulsion

We have often read that horses should move with impulsion—and impulsion is indeed a component of the training scale. But what exactly is meant by impulsion?

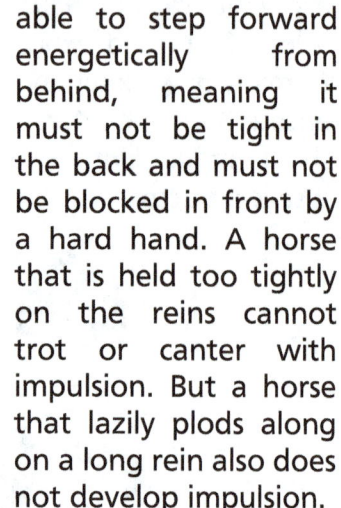

For true impulsion, a horse must be able to step forward energetically from behind, meaning it must not be tight in the back and must not be blocked in front by a hard hand. A horse that is held too tightly on the reins cannot trot or canter with impulsion. But a horse that lazily plods along on a long rein also does not develop impulsion.

Iberian horses can also trot with impulsion when there is good contact and positive tension in the back.

Developing impulsion always requires a strongly pushing hind leg that has already begun to learn how to bear weight. The body needs a positive body tension, which in turn depends on good contact.

NOTE: Impulsion always comes from the hind leg, never from a tense back.

How to train correctly

Basic training for a horse usually includes groundwork: lungeing. On the longe line, young horses get used to the saddle and bridle and begin to learn the rider's voice aids.

NOT LIKE THIS!   BUT LIKE THIS:

Even on the longe line, the fundamentals of the training scale must apply. If the horse is over-tightened when longed, it can no longer move with proper contact or impulsion. The horse in the picture at the top left is over-flexed—its neck and back are tense. Relaxation is no longer possible!

Whether to longe with properly adjusted side reins or with other aids is a matter of opinion. Some horses benefit from correctly fitted auxiliary reins.

With many horses, excellent results can be achieved when lungeing with a plain cavesson. Since the horse's mouth is very sensitive, you should not attach the longe line directly to the bit. A softly padded cavesson is better suited for lungeing.

A cavesson has rings for attaching the longe line. The bit can even be removed entirely.

Collection and Engagement –
All Completely Natural!

Lateral Movements

A horse is naturally able to move straight ahead as well as forward and sideways. Lateral movement does not harm young horses—in fact, it helps them learn to step well under their body with the hind legs. According to the guidelines of the FN (German Equestrian Federation), lateral movements such as shoulder-in, travers (haunches-in), and renvers (haunches-out) are considered exercises that promote collection. Leg-yielding is not classified as a collecting lateral movement.

For simplicity, in this book we refer to all sideways movements as *lateral movements* and distinguish between those that promote suppleness (like leg-yielding) and those that promote collection (like shoulder-in, travers, and renvers).

Lateral movements are excellent for making horses more responsive to your aids and for gymnasticizing the horse. With the help of a good riding instructor, you can learn them yourself too. The prerequisites are that your horse has learned the first three steps of the training scale, and that you have a supple, independent seat.

At the beginning of every riding session, you need to warm up your horse—that means loosening your horse's muscles. To do this, ride at a walk on large, curved lines and post the trot lightly. And once your four-legged friend is trotting forward cheerfully and with impulsion, you can include the first canter.

After this initial warm-up phase, you begin with loosening lateral movements such as leg-yielding and crossing-over. These exercises make your horse more supple, relax the back, and make it more responsive to your leg aids.

However, before you begin with these, you should have a well-balanced seat and a sensitive, refined hand.

> **FACTS**
>
> ALWAYS SIDEWAYS
> The lateral movements include:
> - Leg-yielding (loosening)
> - Shoulder-in (collecting)
> - Travers (collecting)
> - Renvers (collecting)
> - Half-pass (collecting)

When ridden correctly, it looks just as beautiful and harmonious as a free horse in the pasture! (Shown here: leg-yielding at the trot.)

The Half-Pass is also a gymnasticizing lateral movement.

Leg-Yielding

This is a loosening exercise in which the hind leg steps under the body and past the horse's center of gravity. In addition, the horse is flexed at the poll to the inside, with minimal, if any, bend through the body. At the moment the hind leg steps under, the moving femur engages a ligamentary connection to the back, causing it to lift slightly. This leads to relaxation of the back muscles.

If you ride this exercise calmly and with a supple seat, the abdominal muscles—connected via a muscle chain to the lower jaw and hyoid bone—encourage the horse to begin chewing and to relax at the poll. This exercise, together with the shoulder-in, is one of the most important movements for your horse's training.

The benefits of this exercise

Leg-yielding is beneficial for:

- Accustoming the horse to the rider's sideways-driving leg
- Relaxation
- Loosening of the muscles in the back and poll
- Preparation for other exercises such as shoulder-in
- Improvement of contact
- Straightening the horse

Collection can look so light and effortless!

What is Collection?

You've already read that collection is the final point on the training scale. Collection is a form of balance in which the horse shortens its base of support and shifts its center of gravity more to the rear by increasingly bending the large joints of the hind legs during the weight-bearing phase and thereby taking more weight behind.

The rider cannot force collection mechanically. If they try, the horse's back becomes tense—and the exact opposite happens: the horse falls onto the forehand. Many riders believe they are collecting their horse when they pull its head down. They also think they can compress a horse by using a tense driving seat and clamping legs (the "clothespin seat"). Do not do this.

In correct collection, horses should become more aesthetic, more beautiful, and more light-footed. They will also allow the rider to sit more comfortably.

Piaffe of a horse trained according to classical principles.

The engaged, increasingly weight-bearing hindquarters allow the horse to move "uphill." Self-carriage of a naturally elevated horse.

Piaffe of a horse worked "from front to back."

The "activated," forced elevation and the tense, dropped back muscles prevent the hind limbs from stepping under, toward the center of gravity. Tense, choppy steps instead of true collection.

Three illustrations after Professor Schnitzer, 1996

A Comparison of the Results of Different Training Methods

> A piaffe can look impressive! But not every piaffe is truly well ridden—as you can see from the images.
>
> A piaffe is only truly good, and therefore good for the horse, if the hind legs are actually able to step well underneath the body. Then the hindquarters—as riders like to say—"take more weight." The horse appears prouder and taller in front.
>
> The opposite of a beautiful piaffe is when horses stand in place and stomp: the head is held tight, and the hind legs step in place without engagement. Honestly, that's not really beautiful—and for the horses, it's pure coercion!

The Influence of a Horse's Conformation on Its Training

If you look more closely, you'll see that horses not only come in different colors but also have different conformations. Some have long backs, others shorter ones, and some have longer necks than others, and so on. Depending on how a horse is built, certain exercises under saddle are easier for some horses than for others.

> **FACTS**
>
> YOU CAN TELL BY LOOKING AT YOUR HORSE IF IT...
> - ... has been ridden incorrectly over a long period of time.
> - ... has an incorrect, overly high and tight head-neck position and a tense back because it was ridden with strong rein pressure.

A horse with a short neck may have difficulty stretching forward and downward, while one with a short back may not swing as easily with relaxed back muscles. The positioning and angulation of the legs also play a role. A horse with rather straight hind legs cannot bring them as far under its center of gravity, and therefore cannot collect as well as one with better angulation.

Of course, you must always ride a horse according to its body. You must not force it to move in a way that doesn't suit its build. A horse's conformation determines its path of training.

Our sport horses—Warmbloods—generally have a conformation that is very well suited for riding. For decades, they have been bred specifically for their strong aptitude in show jumping or dressage. Depending on their intended use, other breeds have conformations that may make them more or less suited for specific disciplines. These anatomical differences between breeds are the result of centuries of selective breeding.

For example, a riding pony is often just as suitable as a Warmblood for dressage or show jumping. A purebred Arabian is more of a long-distance runner—its favorite discipline is endurance riding. The Haflinger, on the other hand, is usually very well suited for driving, although there are more and more sporty Haflingers who also perform well under saddle in lower-level competitions.

Be considerate of what your horse is capable of, and never ask it to do something it simply cannot do!

One horse for everything? Some horses or ponies are very versatile, while others struggle with certain tasks. Find out what your horse enjoys!

Going on the bit only works without force.
(By the way, the young lady should be wearing a helmet.)

DOES THE HEAD HAVE TO GO DOWN???

If you look around in riding arenas and dressage rings, you often see the same picture: people pulling on the reins, trying to force their horses' heads down. They all believe: *The head has to go down!*

A horse that moves with relaxation should indeed be able to let its neck drop and then seek contact. The difference lies in the fact that a well-ridden horse offers its poll to the rider. In many horses, the rider has simply taken the poll—this is crude force.

To understand the difference, you have to take a very close look at the horse. By now, you've already read a lot about horses and their bodies, and you probably already know:

You cannot ride horses correctly by pulling on their heads! That only makes them sick.

Correct riding is very refined and gentle. No heads are pulled down—because horses with supple backs and actively forward-moving hindquarters will naturally lower their neck and seek the contact.

A beautiful idea, isn't it?

The great thing is that it's actually much easier and much more enjoyable. Because when you ride horses correctly, they also enjoy their work much more and move forward with greater impulsion! And it's a real joy to sit on a horse that moves forward full of energy and snorts contentedly while chewing!

You absolutely must remind yourself: A supple, relaxed seat is the foundation for your horse to be able to develop under you!

Take care of your seat!

Pay attention that your horse's eyes always remain bright and curious...

No Motivation?

We all know that feeling. Sometimes we just don't feel like doing something—and then we do it sloppily or not at all. And sometimes someone annoys us so much that we start thinking about how we could get back at them. That kind of behavior is typical for us humans—but not for horses.

A horse that doesn't perform an exercise correctly has either not understood it or simply can't do it because something is hurting. Horses don't plot how to annoy us or intentionally do things wrong. That's why you should **never punish a horse for a mistake**—it couldn't possibly understand what it's being punished for!

Whether you're riding a young horse that still has a lot to learn and can't concentrate for long yet, or an older one that already knows its job well—**always be considerate of your horse!**

It is always trying its best to please you!

Summary
The Training of Horses

The Training Scale
The training scale is the foundation of the FN riding system.

Contact
Contact must not be forced.

Young Horses
In the first one and a half years, young horses should primarily learn to carry the rider. Rhythm, relaxation, and contact are the initial goals of basic training.

Impulsion
Impulsion always requires active hind legs that push the horse forward from behind.

Basic Training
Basic training includes longeing. But even on the longe line, the principles of the training scale must be followed. Caution: Do not tie your horse's head into a fixed frame when longeing!

Lateral Movements
Lateral movements are excellent for training both rider and horse.

Collection
Collection is the crowning achievement of training and cannot be forced with a harsh hand!

The Influence of Conformation
Be considerate of what your horse is capable of, and never ask for something it cannot do!

"Does the Head Have to Go Down???"
Going "on the bit" only works without force.

No Motivation?
Never punish a horse for a mistake—it's not trying to annoy you on purpose!

Trust is the foundation for a shared future.

Chapter 6
You and Your Horse

Everything that can make you and your horse happy!

Do you like horses? Then you probably enjoy spending time with them too!

In this chapter, you'll find plenty of tips on all the things you can do with horses and ponies. There's actually a whole lot—besides just riding, of course. And even within riding, there are many different things you can try.

The most important thing is that it doesn't get boring—and that it's good for your horse too!

Riding should be fun for both horse and rider!

Basics

Do you remember why you started riding? Maybe because you find horses beautiful and dreamed of riding one across a meadow? Or did you actually dream of riding the same circles in an arena over and over while pulling on the reins? Probably not! But that's exactly what happens in many riding lessons. Sluggish horses plod along in single file, frustrated riding students tug on the reins, and no one is really having fun!

It doesn't have to be that way! There are great riding lessons that are truly enjoyable and where you can learn a lot! This leads to motivated, balanced horses that respond to subtle aids. Take a moment to evaluate your riding lessons (see checklists in the back of this book) to see if they are truly good for you and your horse.

> ## Facts
>
> ### The horse comes first
>
> Riding should be fun not only for you, but also for your horse. For that to happen, your horse has to feel well. Never ride if you suspect your horse might be sick or in pain! A horse that isn't eating or stands listlessly in its stall is probably not feeling well.

What You Need

To ride, you need a horse that is fit and healthy, and a good riding instructor—and beyond that, not much else!

A riding helmet is an absolute must. It should meet safety standards and have a three-point harness to ensure it doesn't slip off in the event of a fall.

You don't need riding breeches for your very first trial lesson—a well-fitting pair of jeans will do. But once you've decided to ride more regularly, riding breeches are very helpful. They don't chafe because they fit more smoothly against the leg and have no inner seams.

Riding boots provide better support in the stirrup and help you keep your leg still against the horse. A great alternative to tall boots are chaps or half-chaps. These are usually made of suede or synthetic leather and are worn around the calf, fastened with Velcro or a zipper.

And what should you wear on top? It should be practical and functional—comfortable t-shirts or sweatshirts are great for riding. However, they shouldn't be too loose, or the instructor won't be able to see your seat properly because everything flaps around.

If you're wearing jodhpur breeches, you can also wear jodhpur boots. These should always have a heel so your foot doesn't slip through the stirrup.

For trail riding, Luise wears the optimal equipment. A spine protector provides safety out on the trail and when jumping.

Even sport horses, like this one, need to go outside every day. Being polished to a high shine alone doesn't make them happy!

The Pasture Is the Best Place to Be

If you could ask horses where they feel happiest, most of them would say: "Out on the pasture!"

There, they can graze all day, move around as much as they want, groom each other's manes, swat flies for one another, and race around together!

The Open Stall

Of course, horses love being on pasture the most—but unfortunately, that's not always possible. We often have too little pasture space, and horses aren't always allowed to graze all day long.

The second-best option—from the horse's point of view—is definitely the horse "shared apartment": the open stall.

In an open stall, horses can move freely between a stable building and a paddock. They can decide for themselves whether they want to play outside, groom each other's manes, or doze in the shelter.

Whether Warmblood, draft horse, or pony—all horses love pasture time!

This type of open stall can be a simple shelter that is closed on three sides and accessible to the horses at all times. It provides protection from rain, heat, or snow. In summer, it can also offer relief from annoying flies—especially if equipped with a fly curtain.

It's also important that there are multiple feeding stations for roughage. Otherwise, a dominant herd leader may hog a huge portion of hay while more timid horses get very little.

If all these conditions are met, an open stall becomes a little horse paradise—with friends and freedom to move around.

The Connemara mares are enjoying life in the herd.

Trail Riding – Page 116

Mounted Games – Page 124

The Richness of Your Possibilities

Driving a Sulky – Page 122

Do you feel like playing the same game every day? Probably not. And it's the same for your horse—it needs variety, or it will get bored! There are so many things you can do with your horse or pony—take a look and see what you both enjoy the most!

Cavalletti work – Page 114

Groundwork – Page 126

Dressage Riding – Page 110

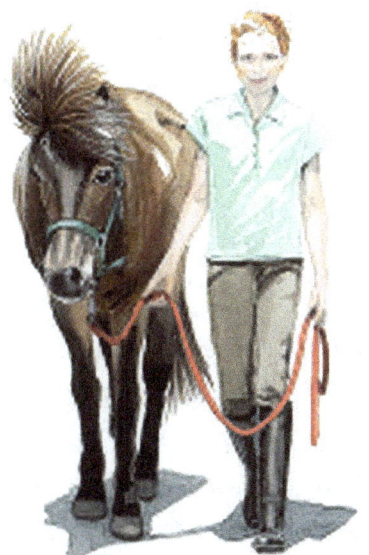

Grooming – Page 108

Going for Walks – Page 120

Show Jumping – Page 112

Hacking Out – Page 118

HEALTHY AND WELL-GROOMED

Grooming is a part of riding. After all, the saddle and bridle shouldn't lie on dirt and cause rubbing. But grooming isn't just about coat care—it's also a way to bond with your horse. At the same time, you check for any minor injuries or scrapes that may need attention.

First, the horse is cleaned of coarse dirt. Use the **curry comb** only on the soft areas of the horse: the neck, belly, and hindquarters.

Areas where the bones are close to the surface—such as the head, legs, and spine—should be cleaned carefully with a **dandy brush**.

Then use a **soft body brush** to clean the head and brush the entire coat again with long strokes. This removes dust from the horse's hair and helps ensure that the horse looks clean and shiny afterward.

Take your time grooming and calmly observe whether your horse is enjoying it.

GROOMING UNTIL IT SHINES

The mane can be combed or brushed, depending on its length. The tail should be groomed by hand—take sections of hair and gently untangle them with your fingers. If you were to brush the tail, you would end up pulling out far too many hairs.

Part of both riding and grooming is picking out the hooves. They must be checked at least once a day. You check whether any stones or pieces of wood have become lodged in the horse's hoof.

The hooves should be inspected daily.

At the same time, check the horseshoes to see if any nails have come loose.

To pick out the hooves, approach the horse from the side and stand facing toward the back. Make your presence known and establish body contact. Place your hand closest to the horse, for example, on its back, and slide that hand slowly from the back over the croup and down the leg. Then, with your inside hand, grasp the horse's leg as low down as possible and clearly say "foot" or "hoof." As soon as the horse lifts its hoof, hold it gently at the fetlock and clean it carefully with a hoof pick.

FACTS

THE FARRIER

Since horses' hooves are constantly growing and often wear down unevenly due to the stress of riding, they need to be regularly checked and trimmed by a farrier. The farrier should come about every 6 weeks to trim or re-shoe the hooves.

Even if everything isn't perfect yet, the young rider is on a good path.

Dressage Riding

What exactly is *dressage riding*?

Dressage riding doesn't just take place at competitions where specific exercises are demonstrated—it's about gymnasticizing the horse so that it can carry its rider with ease.

Dressage includes all exercises that improve the horse's ride-ability and, with it, its health. That's why dressage is also the foundation for show jumping, eventing, and—strictly speaking—even for leisure and endurance riding.

The entire basic training of the horse, the improvement of communication and cooperation between horse and rider—all of that is part of dressage riding.

Not like this!

But like this:

Here, the impulsion flows through a supple back.

Dressage-oriented riding aims to develop the horse's body and mind in such a way that it can respond to the needs of a sensitive rider, allowing for a relationship based on trust and friendship. Psychologically, this means that the horse accepts the rider as a herd leader; it should respect the rider—but not fear them.

Physically, it means that the horse develops in a way that, beyond meeting the basic minimum requirements expected of any healthy horse, it can also meet the specific demands of its discipline—for example, as a leisure, jumping, or endurance horse. This physical development is described by classical riding instructors as a *gymnasticizing process*.

Dressage riding is therefore NOT a special discipline, but the foundation of every serious form of horsemanship.

Jumping is also gymnastics for the horse.

SHOW JUMPING

Show jumping is one of the classic competitive equestrian disciplines. It is very popular because the sporting aspect makes it especially fun. Of course, the principles of good riding always apply.

In show jumping, you especially need a trusting, supple, and well-schooled horse. After all, it's not just about somehow making it around the course.

Your jumping horse, like any dressage horse, must be responsive to the aids and move with suppleness.

You should always wear a safety vest when jumping.

Riding boots provide better support and help you sit more securely!

If you want to jump a course, you need to look toward the next jump as you're landing!

As a rider, you need a good sense of rhythm and a perfect light seat.

You'll also need a healthy dose of courage—because a scaredy-cat rarely becomes a successful show jumper! That said, especially in show jumping, it's important to pay attention to safety. It's better to ride with a safety vest—and of course, you're already wearing a helmet!

FACTS

AT THE COMPETITION

At competitions, there are classes ranging from E to S:
- Class E for *entry-level riders*
- Class A for *beginners*
- Class L for *light*
- Class M for *medium*
- Up to Class S, the *advanced* level.

Cavalletti Work

Cavalletti work is not only a welcome change in the daily routine—it's also very beneficial.

You can use cavallettis in all three gaits. At the walk, they make it easier for horses to move in a stretching posture, promote rhythm, and help horses focus better. Cavalletti work improves relaxation, back swing, and balance.

You always start with low-set cavallettis. More advanced riders and horses can later trot or canter over raised cavallettis. This helps train impulsion and jumping power. For young horses and riders, cavallettis are also a great introduction to jumping. At the trot, however, cavallettis shouldn't be too high, as this risks causing the horse to tense its back and start "hovering."

> **FACTS**
>
> **SPACED OUT**
>
> The distances between cavallettis are approximately:
> - At the walk: about 80 centimeters (32")
> - At the trot: about 1.20–1.40 m (47"-55")
> - At the canter: about 3–4 m (10'-13')

Calmly show your horse the different obstacles.

Cross-Country Riding and Eventing

Eventing was formerly known as "military." It is a discipline in which riders must complete a dressage test, a show jumping course, and a cross-country course. Horse and rider are true all-rounders in this demanding sport—with tremendous jumping ability and a great deal of courage! The cross-country course is especially challenging, where horses must overcome recreated natural obstacles, jump down slopes, handle solid fences, and leap into water.

We're brave enough! A jump over a solid obstacle takes courage!

The cross-country ride is a real challenge for both the rider and their partner, the horse. Both must be in top condition—that's why every eventing competition includes what's called a fitness inspection. Here, a veterinarian checks whether the horse is truly fit and healthy and allowed to participate in the cross-country phase.

Cross-country courses are demanding not just because of the jumps—the length of the course, which is typically ridden at a gallop, requires endurance and strength!

Facts

The Thoroughbred Discipline

Eventing is the signature discipline of Thoroughbreds and Warmbloods with a high proportion of Thoroughbred blood. Their stamina, jumping ability, and courage make Thoroughbreds the winners of major competitions.

Hacking Out

Hacking out is one of the most wonderful things you can do with your horse! Whether you're leisurely strolling through the woods or trotting briskly along country paths—being outdoors is always beautiful!

Of course, there are a few things to keep in mind when riding out. A trail ride always begins at the walk; horses need to be warmed up calmly outside, just like during a dressage session. While you're out, you can trot and canter as long as the ground conditions are good and you're not disturbing pedestrians or cyclists. When you encounter others, you should always transition to the walk.

The walk is also the gait to use when approaching roads—otherwise, it can quickly become dangerous! And naturally, you should always return to the stable at the walk. Or would you want your horse or pony to automatically gallop back to its friends next time?

By the way, besides eventing, there's another outdoor discipline: endurance riding. Riders cover long distances—between 25 and 160 kilometers—in a set time. The goal is to complete the distance as quickly as possible, but speed isn't everything: along the way, a vet regularly checks the horse's health, and the winner is the one whose horse is truly fit and not overworked.

Facts
Safety

As beautiful as it is outside: Always remember to wear your riding helmet and, if possible, a safety vest. Safety comes first. And you should never go riding out alone!

Come on, let's go for a walk!

GRAZING AND WALKING

Horses don't need to be ridden every day. They enjoy a bit of variety, and they'll be happy if you simply take them for a walk. After all, there's so much to discover!

You can walk with your horse or pony through the forest or along grassy paths—and if you feel like it, you can even jog alongside them.

You can also use the walk to introduce your horse to new things and help it become familiar with them.

You can start showing young horses the world by taking them for walks.

Try walking up to that pile of wood with the scary-looking tarp on it, or go take a look at the tractor. If it's not running, you can check it out calmly without your horse getting frightened. For safety, you should always bring an adult along. Always make sure to use a secure lead rope that won't come undone too easily.

Especially with young horses, you can introduce them to many things by leading them by hand. That way, they won't be as fearful during their first ride out. A brave companion can also help a nervous horse become more confident.

It's a good idea to gradually get horses used to grass at the beginning of the pasture season.

Here, even the pony from your earliest childhood still has fun with you!

DRIVING A SULKY

If you want to drive your horse or pony, you should find a qualified driving instructor. Driving courses are offered by all national riding and driving schools, as well as by many local instructors. There, you have the opportunity to learn the fundamentals of carriage driving and, for example, earn the FN driving badges, which are required for participation in driving competitions.

Just like in riding, wearing a helmet while driving is safer!

There are many different types of competitions in driving:

In **dressage driving**, just like in dressage riding, a set test is driven in an arena. It includes specific arena patterns and variations in gaits. These tests are often prerequisites for participating in higher-level driving classes.

In **marathon driving**, a distance of 15 to 18 kilometers is covered. Various sections are evaluated, which must be driven at specific gaits and within certain time limits. The final section contains five to eight obstacles that must be driven through as quickly as possible.

In **obstacle driving**, also called **cones driving**, cones or pylons must be navigated. No cones may be knocked over, nor may any of the balls placed on top be dislodged.

In **cross-country driving**, natural and artificial terrain obstacles—such as bridges, small streams, or narrow, winding paths—must be overcome.

> ## FACTS
> ### ACHENBACH
> The driving system taught in Germany is based on Benno von Achenbach[4]. Achenbach-style driving involves using the correct type of reins, a whip, and a specific method of harnessing.

---

[4] Benno von Achenbach was introduced to carriage driving in the late 1860s. He studied with Howlett in the 1890s, returning several times to gain a greater understanding of the English rein handling system. An accomplished driver himself by this time, Achenbach set out to improve upon Howlett's system. theequineexpert.com - Editor's note.

Mounted games encourage coordination and balance—and are a lot of fun!

Mounted Games

Rider rallies and mounted games offer fun and excitement for every rider. In a rider rally, you usually ride a marked trail in the countryside and complete fun or challenging tasks along the way. These tasks might include hanging laundry from horseback, stacking beer crates, or hitting a ball into a goal with a hockey stick. There are no limits to creativity! Mounted games typically take place in a riding arena: each rider is given different tasks to complete with their horse or pony. Many of these are unusual, and the horse learns to trust its rider in the process.

> **FACTS**
>
> **Confidence Test**
> In the confidence test, the horses are led by hand, and it's observed whether they trust their handler and do not try to flee from unfamiliar objects or situations.

No words needed.

Motivate your horse to stay attentive!

Groundwork

Groundwork is something that many horses really enjoy. You can teach them all sorts of things without anyone sitting on their back. Groundwork is ideal for introducing horses to new experiences.

Almost anything a horse can walk over or be led around is suitable: it can learn to walk over a tarp, bend evenly around cones, carefully walk across a seesaw, place a hoof in an old tire or on a tree stump, step sideways over poles, or back up through a corridor made of poles.

Learning circus tricks is also something many horses truly enjoy!

Summary

You and Your Horse

What you do with your horse should also be beneficial for *your horse*.

What You Need

The most important thing is a **riding helmet!**

The Best Place Is the Pasture

If you asked horses where they feel most comfortable, most would answer: "Out on the pasture!"

The Open Stall

In an open stall, horses can move freely between a shelter and a secured paddock area.

The Variety of Your Options

Horses need variety too.

Healthy and Well-Groomed

Grooming is not just coat care—it's also a way to connect with your horse.

Dressage Riding

Dressage serves to gymnasticize the horse so it can carry its rider with ease.

Show Jumping

The foundation of show jumping is also based on the training scale.

Cavalletti Work

Cavalletti exercises improve looseness, back swing, and balance.

Trail Riding and Eventing

Eventing is a discipline that includes a dressage test, a jumping course, and a cross-country phase.

For cross-country riding, both you and your horse need to be in top shape.

Hacking Out

Hacking out is one of the most enjoyable things you can do with your horse!

Grazing and Walking

Horses don't need to be ridden every day. You can go for walks with your horse or pony through the woods or along grassy paths.

Driving a Sulky

Driving courses are offered by all national riding and driving schools as well as many local instructors.

Mounted Games

Mounted games involve various tasks to complete—from passing through a curtain of streamers to setting a table from horseback.

Groundwork

Groundwork is ideal for introducing horses to new experiences.

The Nine Ethical Principles of the Horse Lover – According to the FN

Do you know the "Ethical Principles of the Horse Lover"? They were published in 1994 by the German Equestrian Federation (FN).

1. Whoever works with a horse takes responsibility for the life entrusted to them.
2. The horse's living conditions must be suited to its natural needs.
3. Both the physical and mental health of the horse must be given top priority, regardless of how it is used.

4. Every human must respect every horse equally, regardless of its breed, age, sex, or whether it is used for breeding, leisure, or sport.

5. Knowledge of the horse's history, its needs, and proper handling is part of our cultural heritage. This knowledge must be preserved, taught, and passed on to future generations.

6. Interacting with horses plays a formative role in personal development, especially for young people. This value must always be recognized and encouraged.

7. Anyone who participates in equestrian sports with a horse is responsible for ensuring both they and the horse undergo proper training. The goal of all training is the greatest possible harmony between human and horse.

8. The use of horses in both competitive and recreational riding, driving, and vaulting must align with the horse's abilities, potential, and willingness to perform. Any attempt to influence a horse's performance through drugs or inappropriate methods is to be rejected and must be punished.

9. A person's responsibility for the horse entrusted to them extends to the end of the horse's life. This responsibility must always be fulfilled in the horse's best interest.

This booklet has been sold well over 100,000 times in just 10 years. And yet, many riders still seem unfamiliar with these principles. But they should be a matter of course for everyone.

We should consciously reconnect with these principles! Riding is a way of life. Ignorance also contributes to poor behavior.

I hope that with this book, we can help bring the FN's ethical principles back into people's awareness.

List of Illustrations, Photographs, and Diagrams

Photos:

Archive	page 11, 16 left, 66, 67, 68 lefts, 96
Candida von Braun	page 50
Sabine Gistl	page 87 right
Petra Herrmann	page 79, 125, U4
Kathrin Hester	page 63, 127
Gerhard Kapitzke	page 68 right
Guillaume Levesque	page 87 left
Private	page 5, 42, 110
Katharina Rücker-Weininger	Title, U2, U3, U4, flap 2-4, page 16 right, 34, 53, 100, 102, 103, 116, 117, 130, Checklist (Horse, Stall)
Jacques Toffi/FN-Archive	Checklist (Riding Teacher)
Sibylle Wiemer	page 10 left

Illustrations: Katharina Rücker-Weininger, www.ruecker-art.de

Note on the illustration on page 88:
The drawing depicts the PRE gelding Galino, owned by Monika Lehmenkühler, www.molekuer.com, photographed by Janine Nielke.

Medical illustrations: Kaja Möbius

Editing and final proofreading: Richard Williams

Copyright for all illustrations and photographs is held by the publisher, Xenophon Press 2025.

Additional Media by Gerd Heuschmann

Collection or Contortion: The Anatomy and Biomechanics of Positioning and Bend ISBN: 978-1948717571

The H.Dv.12 with Commentary: The Rulebook of Riding Culture
ISBN: 9781948717694

Tug of War: Classical Versus "Modern" Dressage ISBN: 978-1570769139

Balancing Act: The Horse in Sport-An Irreconcilable Conflict?
ISBN: 978-1646010721

If Horses Could Speak (DVD): How Incorrect Modern Riding Negatively Affects Horses' Health

Reflections

My thoughts about my riding instructor after reading this book.

_____
_____
_____
_____
_____
_____
_____
_____
_____
_____
_____
_____
_____
_____
_____
_____
_____
_____
_____
_____

My thoughts about my stable after reading this book.

_____
_____
_____
_____
_____
_____
_____
_____
_____
_____
_____
_____
_____
_____
_____
_____
_____
_____
_____

My thoughts about my horse after reading this book.

Xenophon Press Library

www.XenophonPress.com

Xenophon Press is dedicated to the preservation of classical equestrian literature. We bring both new and old works to print.

30 Years with Master Nuno Oliveira, Henriquet 2011

A Journey Through the Horse's Body, Fritz 2012

A Rider's Survival from Tyranny, de Kunffy 2012

A Voice for the Horse, Saint Ryan 2025

Another Horsemanship, Racinet 1994

Academic Art of Riding, Bent Branderup 2024

Austrian Art of Riding, Poscharnigg 2015

Broken or Beautiful: The Struggle of Modern Dressage, Barbier/Conrod 2020

Classic Show Jumping: the de Nemethy Method, de Nemethy 2016

Classical Dressage with Anja Beran, Beran 2021

Collection or Contortion: Anatomy and Biomechanics of Positioning and Bend, Gerd Heuschmann, 2024

Divide and Conquer Book 1, Lemaire de Ruffieu 2016

Divide and Conquer Book 2, Lemaire de Ruffieu 2017

Dressage for the 21st Century, Belasik 2001

Dressage in the French Tradition, Diogo de Bragança 2011

Dressage Principles and Techniques: A Blueprint for the Serious Rider, Tavora 2018

Dressage Principles Illuminated, Expanded Edition, de Kunffy 2021

École de Cavalerie Part II, Robichon de la Guérinière 2015

Elements of Dressage: a Guide for Training the Young Horse, von Ziegner 2022

Equestrian Art: The Collected Early Writings (1951-1956), Nuno Oliveira 2022

Equestrian Art: The Collected Later Works, Nuno Oliveira 2022

Equine Osteopathy: What the Horses Have Told Me, Giniaux 2014

Federico Grisone's "The Rules of Riding," Grisone/Tobey 2023

Fragments from the Writings of Max Ritter von Weyrother, Fane 2017

François Baucher: The Man and His Method, Baucher/Nelson 2013

French Equitation: a Baucherist in America, 1922 & Hand-book for Horsewomen, Bussigny 2023

General Chamberlin: America's Equestrian Genius, Matha 2020

Great Horsewomen of the 19th Century in the Circus, Nelson 2015

Gymnastic Exercises for Horses Volume II, Eleanor Russell 2013

H. Dv. 12 with Commentary, Rulebook of Riding Culture, Heuschman & von Ziegner 2024

Handbook of Jumping Essentials, Lemaire de Ruffieu 2015

Handbook of Riding Essentials, Lemaire de Ruffieu 2015

Healing Hands: Equine Acupressure and First Aid, Giniaux, DVM 1998

Horse Training: Outdoors and High School, Beudant 2014

Horsemanship & Horsemastership Volume 1, US Cavalry 2021

Horsemanship Training Films 3 DVD set, US Cavalry 2021

I, Siglavy, Asay 2018

Journey Through the Horse's Body, Dr. Christina Fritz 2022

Learning to Ride, Santini 2016

Legacy of Master Nuno Oliveira, Millham 2013

Lessons in Lightness: Expanded Edition, Mark Russell 2019

Mark of Clover, Barczy Kelly, 2022

Methodical Dressage of the Riding Horse, Faverot de Kerbrech 2010

Mein Pferd hat die Nase vorn!, Heuschmann 2025

Military Equitation or, A Method of Breaking Horses, and Teaching Soldiers to Ride, Pembroke, and *A Treatise on Military Equitation*, Tyndale 2018

My Horses Have Something to Say, de Wispelaere 2021

My Horse is in front of the Vertical!, Heuschmann 2025

Natural Horsemanship, Based on the papers of a passionate riding instructor, Otto Delacroix 2025

Précis D'Équitation, de Weck 2025

Precise Equitation Manual, de Weck 2025

Principles of Dressage and Equitation, a.k.a. Breaking and Riding, Fillis 2017

Racinet Explains Baucher, Racinet 1997

Releasing the Jaw, Poll, and Neck DVD, Mark Russell 2021

Riding and Schooling Horses, Chamberlin 2020

Riding by Torchlight, Cord 2019

Riding in Rhyme, Davies 2021

Seat, Gaits & Reactions, de Sévy, 2023

Schooling Exercises In-Hand, Hilberger 2009

Science and Art of Riding in Lightness, Stodulka 2015

Shoulder-in: Secret of the Art of Equitation, Salins 2025

Sketches of the Equestrian Art, Barbier/Sauvat 2022

The Art of Riding: Odin at Saumur, Philippe Karl 2024

The Art of Riding a Horse, D'Eisenberg 2015

The Art of Traditional Dressage, Volume 1 DVD, de Kunffy 2013

The Chamberlin Reader, Chamberlin/Matha, 2020

The de Nemethy Method: A training seminar, 8 DVD set, de Nemethy 2019

The Essentials of Captain Charles Raabe's Method of High School Dressage, Decarpentry 2025

The Ethics and Passions of Dressage Expanded Edition, de Kunffy 2013

The Forward Impulse, Santini 2016

The Gymnasium of the Horse, Steinbrecht 2018

The Horses, a novel, Walker 2015

The Italian Tradition of Equestrian Art, Tomassini 2014

The Maneige Royal, de Pluvinel 2010, 2015

The New Method of Dressing Horses a.k.a. A General System of Horsemanship, Cavendish 2020

The Portuguese School of Equestrian Art, de Oliveira/da Costa 2012

The Pure Teachings of Classical Horsemanship, von Neindorff/Simms 2025

The Quest for Lightness in Equitation and Equestrian Questions, Nelson/L'Hotte 2021

The Rider forms the Horse, Udo Bürger & Otto Zietzschmann, 2024

The Rules of Riding Gli Ordini di Cavalcare, Grisone/Tobey 2023

The School of Horsemanship with Egon von Neindorff DVD, 2024

The Spanish Riding School & Piaffe and Passage, Decarpentry 2013

The Spanish Riding School: The Miracle of the White Horse DVD, US Lipizzan Association 2021

To Amaze the People with Pleasure and Delight, Walker 2015

Total Horsemanship, Racinet 1999

Training Hunters, Jumpers, and Hacks, Chamberlin 2019

Training The Flying Changes, Thomas & Shana Ritter 2025

Training Your Foal, Ettl 2022

Training with Master Nuno Oliveira, 2 DVD set, Eleanor Russell 2016

Treasury of Primary Directives for the Equestrian Art, 1720 and Directives, 1898 for the Spanish Riding School of Vienna, Regenthal/Fane, Holbein-Holbeinsberg/Meixner/Williams 2025

Truth in the Teaching of Master Nuno Oliveira, Eleanor Russell 2015

Wisdom of Master Nuno Oliveira, de Coux 2012

12 Answers About Your Riding Instructor

The Checklist – Your Riding Instructor

Here you'll find 12 questions about your riding instructor. On this page are the questions with checkboxes for your answers. On the facing page, you'll find the evaluation.
And now—let's get started!

1 Does your riding instructor make sure you wear a helmet during lessons? ☐ YES ☐ NO	**2** Does your instructor regularly come up with new exercises? ☐ YES ☐ NO	**3** Has your instructor ever explained the horse's body to you in detail? ☐ YES ☐ NO
4 Does he/she check if the saddle and bridle fit and the noseband is loose? ☐ YES ☐ NO	**5** Does he/she ever do lunge lessons with you and correct your seat? ☐ YES ☐ NO	**6** Does your instructor value good cross-country/outdoor riding training? ☐ YES ☐ NO
7 Does he/she explain the purpose of gymnasticizing exercises (e.g. leg-yield)? ☐ YES ☐ NO	**8** Does he/she care about a correctly executed stretching posture? ☐ YES ☐ NO	**9** Does your instructor ride without auxiliary reins or draw reins? ☐ YES ☐ NO
10 Does your horse usually go with its nose in front of the vertical? ☐ YES ☐ NO	**11** Does he/she explain the effects of rough rein aids? ☐ YES ☐ NO	**12** Is your instructor calm and friendly? ☐ YES ☐ NO

Now count how many times you answered YES and how many times you answered NO. You'll find the evaluation of this test on the back of this sheet.

YES: ☐
NO: ☐

12 Answers About Your Riding Instructor

The Evaluation – Your Riding Instructor

You answered the questions to the best of your knowledge and counted all your YES and NO answers? Great! Now you're about to find out how well your horse is really doing—here comes the evaluation:

You Answered YES 0-3 Times:

Please finish your current set of riding lessons as quickly as possible. This is definitely not the kind of instruction that benefits you or your horse. It's best to evaluate your next riding instructor right away using this checklist.

You Answered YES 4-8 Times:

Talk to your riding instructor about all the questions you had to answer with NO. If they are truly a good instructor, over time you'll be able to answer YES to all of them.

You Answered YES 9-12 Times:

Fantastic – we'd love to meet this riding instructor with you!

Instructors this good deserve to be recommended, because many other riders are looking for someone just like this!

So go ahead and snap a photo of this checklist and email it along with your name and your riding instructor's address to:

Dr. Gerd Heuschmann
c/o XenophonPress@gmail.com
Xenophon Press 7518 Bayside Road
Franktown, Virginia 23354, USA

12 QUESTIONS THAT BRING YOU CLOSER TO YOUR HORSE

THE CHECKLIST - YOUR HORSE

Here you'll find 12 questions about your horse. On this page are the questions with checkboxes for your answers. On the facing page, you'll find the evaluation. And now—let's get started!

1 Can your horse be saddled and bridled calmly? ☐ YES ☐ NO	2 Does your horse have well-maintained, properly shaped hooves? ☐ YES ☐ NO	3 Does your horse stand still when mounting until you're ready to ride? ☐ YES ☐ NON
4 Do you do more than just dressage and jumping with your horse? ☐ YES ☐ NO	5 Do you ride your horse out once or twice a week? ☐ YES ☐ NO	6 Is your horse in good feeding and grooming condition? ☐ YES ☐ NO
7 Can your horse be touched and groomed all over its body without issues? ☐ YES ☐ NO	8 Can your horse be controlled at all time while being led? ☐ YES ☐ NO	9 When cleaning hooves, does your horse calmly and easily give each one? ☐ YES ☐ NO
10 Does your horse remain calm when trail riding, even in unfamiliar situations? ☐ YES ☐ NO	11 Does your horse load into the trailer without problems? ☐ YES ☐ NO	12 Can your horse be led away from other horses without resistance? ☐ YES ☐ NO

Now count how many times you answered YES and how many times you answered NO. You'll find the evaluation of this test on the back of this sheet.

12 Answers That Bring You Closer to Your Horse

The Evaluation – Your Horse

You answered the questions to the best of your knowledge and counted all your YES and NO answers? Great! Now you'll find out how well your horse is really doing—here comes the evaluation:

You Answered Yes 0–3 Times:

You and your horse probably haven't been a team for very long. Like any friendship, it takes time to grow. Your horse still has little trust in you and is signaling that many things aren't quite right. Please seek professional help to check everything—saddle, bridle, health, environment, and feed.

You Answered Yes 4–8 Times:

You and your horse have already built a good foundation. But to become a perfect team, you need a few more YES answers. Take a close look at the questions you answered with NO—those reveal important messages your horse is trying to send you. These are the areas you need to work on. Talk to your riding instructor; they will be happy to help you.

You Answered Yes 9–12 Times:

You and your horse—a great match! But even in a strong relationship, you always need to keep working on your connection and never become careless. The saddle should be checked regularly for fit, and your horse might have an important message for you tomorrow—stay attentive and always observe your horse closely...

12 QUESTIONS THAT BRING YOU CLOSER TO YOUR HORSE

THE CHECKLIST - YOUR STABLE

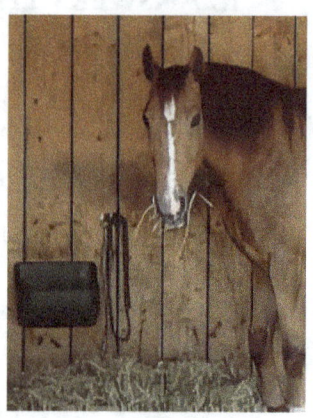

Here you'll find 12 questions about your horse. On this page are the questions with checkboxes for your answers. On the facing page, you'll find the evaluation.

And now—let's get started!

1 Does your horse go out to pasture in the summer? ☐ YES ☐ NO	2 Does your horse go outside even in bad weather or during winter? ☐ YES ☐ NO	3 Does your horse get enough hay so that it always has something to chew on? ☐ YES ☐ NO
4 Is your horse's stall at least 3 meters by 4 meters in size? ☐ YES ☐ NO	5 Can your horse see the horses to the left and right of its stall? ☐ YES ☐ NO	6 Does your horse have a paddock stall with a small outdoor area? ☐ YES ☐ NO
7 Is your horse kept in an open stall with other horses? ☐ YES ☐ NO	8 Are the horses in box stalls fed at least three times a day? ☐ YES ☐ NO	9 Is cleanliness maintained in your stable? (in the aisles, courtyard, etc.) ... ☐ YES ☐ NO
10 Does the ceiling height of the stable ensure good, fresh air? ☐ YES ☐ NO	11 Does your horse have several hours of contact with other horses each day? ☐ YES ☐ NO	12 Are the horses checked multiple times a day (colic risk)? ☐ YES ☐ NO

Now count how many times you answered YES and how many times NO. You'll find the evaluation of this test on the back of this sheet.

YES: ☐
NO: ☐

12 Answers That Will Hopefully Make Your Horse Happy

The Evaluation – Your Stable

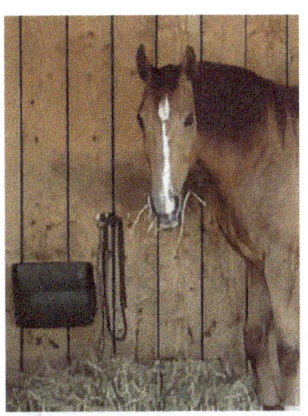

You answered the questions to the best of your knowledge and counted all your YES and NO answers? Great! Now you'll find out how well your horse is really doing—here comes the evaluation:

You answered YES 0–3 times:

Your stable is probably a really nice place for you, and you've made great friends there. But your horse might not feel as comfortable as you do. Horses should be able to spend time with other horses every day, be outdoors as much as possible, and receive plenty of roughage like hay. Talk to your parents and consider whether it might be better to look for a different stable.

You answered YES 4–8 times:

Your stable is making a good effort to keep horses in a way that supports their well-being. Take a closer look at what could still be improved. Your horse should really be able to spend time with other horses every day, go outside regularly, and get plenty of roughage. Is there a way to improve that?

You answered YES 9–12 times:

Wow! Your horse is lucky—it's in a stable where it truly feels good! We'd love to know where such great stables are so we can recommend them to others... that helps all horses!

So go ahead and snap a photo of this checklist and send it along with your name and your stable's address to Gerd Heuschmann c/o XenophonPress@gmail.com

Copyright 2025 Xenophon Press Franktown, Virginia, USA
Richard Williams Publisher Xenophon Press LLC 1-757-442-1060
www.XenophonPress.com

Author Biography

Dr. Gerhard Heuschmann was born on October 6, 1959, in Marktredwitz, Germany, and grew up on his family's farm.

After completing his secondary education in 1979, he underwent training at the German Riding School in Warendorf. He then went on to study veterinary medicine at the Ludwig Maximilian University of Munich. After graduating, he initially worked as an assistant veterinarian in Munich before taking a position in 1989 as a junior staff member at the German Equestrian Federation (FN) in Warendorf. Shortly afterward, Dr. Heuschmann assumed the role of advisor in the breeding department. His collaboration with the FN ended in 1991.

In that same year, he took over an equine clinic in North Rhine-Westphalia. From 1991 to 1994, Dr. Heuschmann ran the clinic together with Dr. Baltus and simultaneously developed what has since become his renowned lecture series on equine biomechanics.

In 2006, his first publication, *"Finger in der Wunde"* (*"Tug of War"*), was released and has since been translated into 15 languages. This successful debut was followed by other works, including *"Balanceakt"* (*"Balancing Act"*), *"Stellung und Biegung"* (*"Positioning and Bending"*), and the DVD *"Stimmen der Pferde"* (*"If Horses could Speak"*). These titles are also now available in multiple languages. His newest book is a commentated version of the classic, *H. Dv. 12* where he and Kurd Albrecht von Ziegner give valuable insights for todays riders: *H. Dv. 12 with Commentary*.

Dr. Heuschmann remains active worldwide as a speaker at symposia and as a trainer at numerous seminars and training events.

www.ingramcontent.com/pod-product-compliance
Lightning Source LLC
Chambersburg PA
CBHW081433070526
44586CB00020B/2573